LAWYER PROFESSIONALISM

LAWYER PROFESSIONALISM

Jack L. Sammons, Jr.

CAROLINA
ACADEMIC
PRESS
POST BOX 51879
DURHAM
N. CAROLINA
27717

LAWYER PROFESSIONALISM

Copyright © 1988 Jack L. Sammons, Jr.
All rights reserved

Carolina Academic Press
P.O. Box 51879
Durham, North Carolina 27717
(919) 489-7486

LC Number 87-73172
ISBN 0-89089-324-1 Paper
ISBN 0-89089-323-3 Cloth

Printed in the United States of America

Cover and text design by C. Mayapriya Long

To my parents,
Jack and June Sammons

shadow of law

law

"The truth is that the right administrator of law to conduct is the person whose conduct is involved, and really that's the way we go on and carry on the practical affairs of the world. The man or the woman . . . , the person whose conduct is to be affected by law is the one to administer the law, and, when that is done, of course no court is ever called on, and no outsider has anything to do with it. That's the true government, and the only sort there ought to be, and the only sort there would be if people would govern themselves accordingly. I believe that this theory is sound in itself, and I believe it leads to this consequence and conclusion, that there is a foundation of an order of nobility. I believe there ought to be, if it were practicable, a distinction made among people, based on that fact—that those people who govern themselves and don't need any other government, are noble and ought to be recognized as nobles. They are lords, not to govern others, but by reason of the fact that they govern themselves. That is the true order of nobility—self government. That's what I believe. I think there is no other true order. The other orders are all artificial, and what you might call fanciful."

From: "Some Revised Thoughts
of an Old Man—An Old Lawyer"
Address by Judge Logan E. Bleckley
to the Georgia Bar Association,
July 6, 1905.
(Stenographically reported)

Law is implemented not based on what it is but on what people think it is

CONTENTS

PREFACE

One way or another, sometime during your three years of law school, or immediately thereafter, you will form a conception of what it means to be a member of the legal profession. In doing so, you will acquire an image of how a professional conducts himself or herself. The conception may be incomplete and the image may not be well defined, but a conceptual framework will be there and, once in place, it will be important to you and difficult to change.

Unfortunately, the process by which you will form this conception will not be a conscious one for the most part. In fact, the process will probably resemble unconscious imitation more than it does thoughtful reflection. There are many reasons for this, and none of them is good. The purpose of this book is to make the process a more conscious one.

It has been my experience that the questions you need to ask as a law student or a new lawyer about the profession and professionalism in order to make this process a conscious one seem to get lost in the first years of law school and, by the time they have been found, so much has been acquired by imitation that the questions have lost much of their force for you. In this introduction to professionalism I try to ask the questions for you and to do so in a way which prompts a response from you.

The form of the book is a dialogue of questions and answers. I hope this form encourages you to start your own dialogue on the subject—your own internal dialogue, if nothing else. Of course, there will be questions you would have asked which I do not, and many of the answers I provide to the questions

I do ask will not satisfy you. Those are the places where your dialogue begins. Later, you may find that some of the answers which satisfied you at first no longer satisfy you. Those are the places where your dialogue continues.

A word of warning—do not let the form of the book mislead you. This book is intended to be read straight through from beginning to end. None of the answers to individual questions are independent of other questions and other answers. You cannot pick a question which interests you, for whatever reason, read the answer and expect to learn much of anything of any use to you. After reading the book straight through, if there is a particular topic you wish to explore further, look at the articles and books noted in the footnotes and start your exploration there.

You should read this book very critically. The question and answer form should encourage you to do that. You do not need to have any particular knowledge about the law, the practice of law, or ethics in order to be a critical reader. As an author of a work like this one, I offer you one great advantage for critical reading. I am not an authority. You do not need to give me the respect that you would give to an authority. You are free to disagree with me without having to consider my position of authority. You can use your own mind; you do not need to borrow mine. At the very heart of it, the questions asked here about the practice of law are reducible to everyday problems well within the grasp of all of us. These are not questions reserved for specialists, although specialists often claim them as their own. I hope you will trust your own capacity to think through the problems that really matter.

The answers to the questions asked in the book offer my conception of professionalism based on, and in response to, the work of many others. I offer you my conception, rather than a survey of different ones, because I believe that offering one reasonably clear and coherent conception of professionalism is the best way to provoke your thinking on the subject. I have tried to give you something definite to respond to. I want to warn you, however, that there are other conceptions of professionalism you should consider. The questions asked here are much too important to leave to one person. You will have missed the point of this book if you leave them to me.

ACKNOWLEDGMENTS

I do not think that there is an original thought in this book. At least, I hope not. It was not my intention to formulate a new conception of professionalism for lawyers, but to offer to readers new to the subject what I judged to be the best thoughts on it woven into one reasonable conception and presented in a readable fashion which encourages response. Accordingly, there are many more people to thank than those who have been mentioned in footnotes following the rules of attribution. Here is a partial list of those who may recognize the products of their thinking in this book in action or in reaction. To each, it is my hope that I have done no disservice: J. Auerbach, M. Bayles, D. Binder, D. Campbell, E. Cahn, R. Condlin, R. Cort, M. Davis, A. Donagan, J. Finnis, M. Frankel, M. Freedman, C. Fried, G. Hazard, D. Hudson, A. Kaufman, K. Kipnis, D. Landon, W. Lehman, D. Luban, M. Mindes, T. Morgan, J. Noonan, L. Patterson, T. Porterhouse, G. Postema, S. Price, J. Raz, R. Redmount, D. Rhodes, D. Richards, D. Rosenthal, R. Rotunda, T. Schneyer, D. Schön, M. Schwartz, T. Shaffer, W. Simon, R. Solomon, M. Spiegel, J. Stanley, R. Stevens, S. Stoljar, J. Thibault, L. Walker, R. Wasserstrom, B. Williams, C. Wolfram, and all those responsible for the drafting of the Stanley Report on Professionalism for the ABA Commission on Professionalism.

I am deeply indebted to Gus Cleveland, Deryl Dantzler, Monroe Freedman, Fred Gedicks, Mark Harrison, Tom Morgan, Robert Redmount, Ivan Rutledge, Tom Shaffer, Richard Solomon, Justin Stanley, and Rex Stevens, for comments on an earlier draft. The parts of this book which please me most are all a product of those comments. In my correspondence with Professor Shaffer, I have learned from him, once again, what it means to be a gentleman.

I am very grateful to the many colleagues at Mercer Law School who offered me their thoughts and their encouragement and to the students of the Law School who provided me with most of the questions and many of the answers. I am also very grateful to Sabrina C. Balkcom who devoted many hours of fine work to the preparation of the original manuscript.

Finally, anyone familiar with the writings of James Pike, Tom Shaffer, Monroe Freedman and Charles Fried will know immediately how much I owe to them. Professor Freedman's hypotheticals are quoted with permission of the author.

Jack L. Sammons, Jr.
Macon, Georgia, and
Windsor, Vermont
1987

LAWYER
PROFESSIONALISM

· ONE ·

A PROFESSIONAL IDEAL

What is professionalism?

The generally accepted concept is that professions provide particular types of services to others and professionalism is doing that in a manner which approaches a professional ideal. The professional ideal must be something other than a benefit to the professional. In other words, we can expect more of a professional than that.[1] The ideal must offer an acceptable justification for the activities of the profession.

This is a very general definition, and it leaves to others the difficult task of determining which occupations can legitimately be called professions.[2]

---

1. A. Goldman, *The Moral Foundations of Professional Ethics* 18 (1980).

2. The A.B.A. Commission on Professionalism explored this question. *See* " '.... In The Spirit of Public Service:' A Blueprint For The Rekindling of Lawyer Professionalism," *American Bar Association Commission On Professionalism* (1986). The Commission's comments may be useful:

"[T]he Commission believes ... [t]he practice of law 'in the spirit of a public service' can and ought to be the hallmark of the legal profession.

More recently, others have identified some common elements which distinguish a profession from other occupations. Commission member Professor Eliot Freidson of New York University defines our profession as:

An occupation whose members have special privileges, such as exclusive licensing, that are justified by the following assumptions:

1. That its practice requires substantial intellectual training and the use of complex judgments.

2. That since clients cannot adequately evaluate the quality of the

3

The word "professionalism" has bad connotations for many people. For some it means getting paid for not getting upset when you should. For others it means wearing a three-piece suit to do the grocery shopping, or using an interior decorator to select your oversized mahogany desk. If the word only carries connotations like those for you, I ask that you give it a second chance.

Why isn't professionalism just doing a good job of providing a professional service? Why do we need to identify a professional ideal?

The simple answer is that the professional ideal tells us what a good job is. For example, you probably know that lawyers have professional obligations to their clients to keep certain information confidential and to avoid serving interests which conflict with the interests of their clients. The profession has rules which attempt to define minimum compliance with these obligations, but what is more than the minimum? If the rules of the profession are minimum obligations, what is the lawyer to aspire to beyond that minimum? Which side of the lines drawn by the rules is the aspirational side? Which side constitutes doing "a good job?" The professional ideal provides the direction needed to answer that question.

Of course, the need for direction is not just at the level of the individual practitioner. The need is there at higher organizational levels as well. For example, law schools, among

---

service, they must trust those they consult.

3. That the client's trust presupposes that the practitioner's self-interest is overbalanced by devotion to serving both the client's interest and the public good, and

4. That the occupation is self-regulating—that is, organized in such a way as to assure the public and the courts that its members are competent, do not violate their client's trust, and transcend their own self-interest."

The Commission's notes tell us that Professor Freidson's definition was prepared especially for the Report.

other things, are supposed to introduce you to the practice of law, but this socialization process presupposes some clarity about the group into which you are being socialized.[3] To what should law schools aspire in the socialization process for new lawyers? You need some sense of a professional ideal to answer that question.

The rest of society also needs to know to what we aspire in order to evaluate our performance as a profession and to decide how important we are in comparison with other needs and other services.

Another way of saying all of this is that the professional ideal defines us as lawyers. If it is a moral ideal, it also provides the moral justification for who we are and what we do as lawyers.

That sounds logical, but I am not convinced. It may be that muddling through all those decisions without some over-all sense of direction is good enough. But let's go on with your idea and see where it goes. Maybe we can come back to the need for a professional ideal question. What is our professional ideal?

There may be more than one. In fact, most lawyers and academicians speak and write as if there were several. I think, however, that we should stick with one if we can find one that does all we want an ideal to do. We can always add others if we get into trouble. There are, of course, many ways of expressing the one that I think most people would start with.

O.K., but answer the question. What is our professional ideal?

My way of expressing it is that we make it possible for people to participate in a meaningful fashion in the resolution

---

3. D. Campbell, *Doctors, Lawyers, Ministers: Christian Ethics In Professional Practice* 29 (1982). *See also* Wasserstrom, "Legal Education and the Good Lawyer," 34 *J. Legal Educ.* 155 (1984).

of their social disputes or in the prevention of social disputes or both.[4] Service to that ideal of meaningful participation defines our profession and the moral value of meaningful participation justifies it.

Is that an ideal for everything that lawyers do? Is it an ideal for public disputes as well as private ones?

Yes, it is. Every task lawyers perform involves the prevention or resolution of social disputes. If you prefer, think of social disputes as involving all those forms of conduct about which society has decided it may have something to say.

I thought you were going to say that our professional ideal has something to do with serving truth and justice or, at least, protecting individual rights?

There are certainly other ideals you could add to your list: healing relationships, peacemaking, individual freedom, and serving as a buffer between the individual and society. I think that the values in other ideals are either served by the one ideal I offer or are so inconsistent with it that they are values which the profession cannot serve. You will have to be the judge of my assertion of one ideal after we have finished talking about this. You may find, as I do, that everything you want to accomplish by positing other ideals is accomplished by this one.

I will keep that in mind, but first, don't people participate in their disputes without lawyers?

Yes, but when the norms applied to resolve the disputes and the processes involved become too complex, it is impos-

---

4. This description is elaborated upon in Sammons, "Participation, Process, and the Practice of Law," *Law & Relig.* ____ (1988) [hereinafter "Participation"].

sible to participate in a meaningful way without specialized knowledge and specialized skills. That is where we come in.

Do lawyers really function in society in the way you have described?

I don't know. The ideals of a profession and of professionalism *can* become no more than self serving myths in practice. That danger is always there. I am talking about an aspirational professional ideal. We may or may not be failing in our effort to meet it, but it still governs us.

You said that if a professional ideal is a moral ideal then it provides moral justification for what we do as professionals? How is your professional ideal of meaningful participation a moral ideal?

Meaningful participation means that the client's participation will reflect, and reflect upon, the person of the client in the dispute. In other words, only through participation can the client be an "author of his own life" in the dispute.

There are many ways of describing that as a moral ideal with important differences in the descriptions, for example, "respect for persons," "human dignity," "individual liberty" and "freedom." As used here, the concept of being "an author of your own life"—autonomy, in other words—as a moral ideal is a derivative. Its morality is derived from the moral assertion that there is unique moral value in what it means to be you.[5]

---

5. The assertion that there is moral value in what it means to be you has a very good pedigree in moral philosophy, but I am both incapable of giving a full explication of that and not inclined to do so here. There are many ways of understanding the metaphysics of that moral assertion. Those ways range from seeing it as a religious statement, as I do, to seeing it as confirmation of the motto of the citizens of Lake Woebegon: "Sumus quod sumus." G. Keilor, *Lake Woebegon Days* (1985). A further discussion of this assertion is found in the Appendix, part 1.

Autonomy is a necessary condition for "what it means to be you."

That is what our professional ideal says to people when it offers meaningful participation, and that is its morality.

I understand the value to the individual. Is there value to the society?

Yes, there is, but we need to be careful in talking about it.

Why?

Because it is very easy to start thinking that we provide meaningful participation in order to accomplish some social purpose other than meaningful participation. The "meaningful" of meaningful participation is meaning to the person; not to the society.

The notion of affording personal autonomy in order to serve some collective good is a confusing one at best. It may be best to say that a society which values personal autonomy for its own sake benefits from having it provided. But all of that aside, there are substantial benefits to society in meaningful participation because of the nature of the processes we use to develop meaningful participation within what the client brings to the relationship.

What do you mean?

Well, the problem-solving and decision-making processes we go through with our clients are good processes from society's point of view and, cumulatively, these processes produce good results for society.

What is good about those processes?

The processes produce richly connected thinking about the problems, and the client's decisions about these problems are well informed. The particular processes we follow are systematic ones akin to classical reasoning. When we are functioning as we should, that is, when we are trying to reflect the person of the client, we assist the client in exploring many alternative definitions of the problems; we identify and develop the information needed to clarify those definitions and to distinguish among them; we assist the client's exploration of alternative solutions through a consideration of a very broad range of consequences for each solution, including legal consequences, moral consequences, social consequences, economic consequences, and psychological consequences; and we assist in the evaluation of each solution by clarifying client values and so forth.[6]

These processes keep the client and the lawyer tentative about the dispute and tentative about the ends of the representation, which is essential if the client is to continue to participate. The client and the lawyer are constantly reflecting on the ends of the representation and, in doing so, they are constantly redefining what it means to be a lawyer for this client in this dispute.[7]

How is that good from society's point of view?

Please understand that when I say "society" I am talking about a society like the one in which we are living. The answer to your question is too difficult for me if I try to talk about "society" in the abstract.

Much of the good of the processes, from society's point of view, is the cumulative effect of individuals thinking about

---

6. This description of the problem-solving process is derived from Cort & Sammons, "The Search for 'Good Lawyering': A Concept and Model of Lawyering," 29 *Clev. St. L. Rev.* 397 (1980); reprinted in 1 *Antioch LJ.* 7 (1981), and *ALI-ABA CLE Review*, Vol. 31 (Nos. 1-6) (1982). The assertion that these processes produce "richly connected" thinking is supported in "Participation", *supra* note 4.

7. *See generally* D. Schön, *The Reflective Practitioners—How Professionals Think In Action* (1983).

their disputes in this way. Quite obviously, the way in which people think about their disputes with each other is important to the society. In fact, I think it is fair to say, that it defines it.

When we are functioning as we should, our clients' thinking includes consideration of the society, of its norms—particularly its legal ones—and of the other people in the dispute. Those are things that society needs people to think about carefully. For example, if society wants to accomplish anything through its legal norms, then it must have those norms considered by individuals in thinking through disputes.

This is sketchy, I know, and I would like to leave it that way for now because I believe that some of the other social values will pop-up in context as we continue our conversation. Some of those values are dependent on what I described as "reflecting on the ends of the representation."

What do you mean by "reflecting on the ends of the representation?

The lawyer and the client stay open about what the client wants. Both recognize that the ends of the representation are complex and that they are ambiguous.[8] For example, some have said that winning is the end of all legal representation. But what does winning mean? If it is the maximization of self interest, for example, then we have to go back to the complexities of the person to determine what self interest is in a particular dispute. Even in its simplest sense "winning" does not describe what is foremost with most clients because there are many things they won't do simply to win. "Winning" is a complex and ambiguous end.

---

8. *See generally* C. Fried, *An Anatomy of Values: Problems Of Personal and Social Choice* (1970).

But what if a client comes in knowing exactly what he or she wants? How is that ambiguous? For example, the client says: "I want a bankruptcy." Shouldn't I just accept that as the end of the representation? The rest of it is not my business, is it? In fact, isn't it paternalistic for me to make the client question his or her initial decision?

I don't think so. I believe that we can assume that our clients know what they want, intend to get it (in other words, it is not just a wish), and are willing to discuss it.[9] The gist of this is that there is nothing inconsistent with personal autonomy in being willing to listen to others and to subject the thinking behind the intended end to friendly scrutiny.[10]

Practically, in your example, the client has chosen the bankruptcy without an awareness of alternatives and without knowledge of the legal consequences of his choice. Thus, part of what will happen to him is not something he or she has consciously chosen, but could have. By providing awareness of alternatives and knowledge of consequences, you are increasing the client's autonomy, not diminishing it.

In terms of the problem-solving process I described before, the client who comes in the office asking for a bankruptcy is like a patient who asks for an appendectomy. You don't start the process with the solution.

This is all part of "your business," as you put it. Pursuing the bankruptcy, in your example, or the will, or the divorce, or the judgment, or whatever solution has been chosen by the client, is not representing the person of the client and rep-

---

9. R. Stevens, *Kant on Moral Practice: A Study Of Moral Success and Failure* 143 (1981) (interpreting *Anthropologie* 8:117-18; Gregor, at 95-97.) The fourth assumption, that the client recognizes the limitation of the social setting, is discussed infra. *See also* Raz's description of personal autonomy in J. Raz, *The Morality Of Freedom* 369-429 (1986): "[The ideal of autonomy] requires that self creation must proceed, in part, through choice among an adequate range of options; that the agent must be aware of his options and the meaning of his choices . . . ." *Id.* at 389-90.

10. *See also* D. Campbell, *supra* note 3, at 62.

resentation of the person is essential to meaningful participation.

What if the client does not want to make any decision?
What do you do about clients who want to abdicate respon-
sibility for decisions to you? How can you represent the per-
son of the client in that situation?

First, we are talking about those decisions which matter
to your client. We make it possible for people to participate
in their disputes, but the level of that participation must
depend, in part, on what matters to the client.

Second, clients cannot totally abdicate responsibility for
decisions to me because they remain legally and morally
responsible for them. To the extent that they do, however, I
would make it clear that I am now the one participating and
that the participation will reflect my values. I think you will
find that those decisions which require your professionalism
are also decisions which matter to your client.

O.K. Can we get back to our main topic? I think you are
saying that being a professional means accepting an obli-
gation to provide meaningful participation to our clients,
and that we serve the individual and the society by doing
that. Are there any other professional obligations we have to
accept?

Wait! I want to quibble with what you have said. The
professional ideal was to "make it possible for people to participate, etc." The ideal is broader than the obligation to the
client you have described. Also, as you may already know, I
don't like anything which implies that there is a clean distinction between the individual and the society.

· TWO ·

PROFESSIONAL OBLIGATIONS

Now to answer the question. Yes, there are other professional obligations, but I think they all have as a source the professional ideal of meaningful participation. The obligations are inherent in the nature of serving clients in a manner which approaches this ideal.

What are they?

Is it O.K. if I just give some examples rather than trying to cover everything at one time?

Yes.

To start with, you described an obligation to clients, and that prompted a reaction from me because the professional ideal implies an obligation to people before they become clients. For example, it implies an obligation to make your services available to people. Our profession has long recognized specific professional obligations, incumbent upon every lawyer, of pro bono representation of clients and of representing clients without consideration of the popularity of the client or the client's cause. These specific professional obligations are derived from the general professional obligation to make your services available. These are not matters of charity, but of duty in service to the professional ideal.

What is pro bono representation?

Pro bono representation is the representing of clients without charging a fee. It is one way of making our services available to those who cannot afford it.

But our services are not really available to huge segments of the population.

I think you are correct. In part, the fault is ours for failing to live up to our professional obligation. There are, however, obvious limits on the professional obligation. The obligation of the individual attorney is to provide representation without a fee, to the extent that can be consistent with maintenance of a practice. Anything beyond that is obviously self-defeating for the professional ideal. The extent that pro bono representation is consistent with practice is determined, in part, by society's decisions about the allocation of resources and so forth. Also, remember that we are talking about ideals here. I hope you are not put off by that. At the end of all this, we can ask, if you want to, whether or not the ideal is realistic enough to serve us as an ideal.

O.K., but I do want to ask one more question which may be along the same lines. You said that our professional ideal of meaningful participation implies a professional obligation to people to make our services generally available. Hasn't our profession reduced the availability of our services with restrictions on advertising and solicitation of clients, and, if so, how do you reconcile those restrictions with our professional ideal?

That question has been a traumatic one for the profession. There are some in the profession who view any advertising or solicitation as inconsistent with professionalism, and some who view any restraints on advertising or solicitation as inconsistent with it. I think, in answering your question, that we should try applying our description of the professional ideal to a hypothetical involving some of the remaining restraints on solicitation to see if those restraints are, or are not, consistent with the ideal. In doing so, I think that I can clarify much of what has been said so far, and, perhaps, anticipate other questions.

This particular hypothetical is from Professor Monroe Freedman.[1] In my opinion, Professor Freedman, through his hypothetical, is doing more than anyone else to provoke clear thinking about the meaning of our profession.

"Laura Eagle is a sole practitioner in a large city. One evening an acquaintance who is a social worker mentioned to Laura the horrible conditions he had seen that day on a visit to a private nursing home in the city—filth, poor food, and neglect, even to the point of one patient who had maggots growing in her flesh. Because the patients are poor, elderly, and bedridden, and are rarely visited by anyone, they have no way to help themselves or to get help.

"Laura offered the social worker $100.00 if he would return to the nursing home, explain to some of the patients about the possibility of a class action on their behalf, and sign up one or more of them on a contingent fee. Laura made it clear that the social worker was not to mislead or pressure the patients in any way, and he followed her instructions.

"As a result, Laura became attorney for the patients and obtained a substantial recovery for them and a court order protecting their rights to adequate care. She also received a substantial fee on the normal one-third contingency basis.

"At Laura's disciplinary hearing she admitted that a significant motive for her taking the case was to earn the fee. She pointed out that she could not have afforded to handle such a difficult and time-consuming case on a *pro bono* basis. She preferred representing the patients, but, if someone else had been representing the patients, she would have been willing

---

1. M. Freedman, *Two Fables for Lawyers, Fable I—The Spirit of Public Service* (1987).

to represent the nursing home operators....[S]he said ... 'I believe in the English barrister [cab rank] practice of taking the next client in line.' "

This hypothetical is designed, in part, to challenge the profession's restrictions on solicitation of clients. What harm has been done here by her violation of those restrictions other, perhaps, than some harm to the vague notion of the dignity of the profession? If we are justified not by the dignity of our social status, but by the dignity of our service to people, how can we justify imposing sanctions upon Laura for being "of service?"

The problem with that challenge is that it misconceives the nature of the "service." The service we provide is meaningful participation by clients in the prevention or resolution of their disputes; it is not the securing of benefits—or rights, for that matter—which we posit as the ends of the representation. The solicitation restrictions, understood in light of our professional ideal, are designed to protect the client-lawyer relationship in its formation. Ideally, the client should initiate the relationship, freely and intelligently, because even in its conception, the relationship is about client participation. Initiation by the client is important for participation because the relationship is defined anew each time it is formed. This formation is inherent in the notion of "reflecting on the ends of the representation." The client determines, in part, what it means to be a lawyer for this client. Lawyer initiation runs the grave risk of confusing and distorting what the relationship is about because the client has less say in it. That is what happened here.

Come on now. Surely there is nothing wrong with assuming these folks want something done about the nursing home.

Perhaps not, but is *this* what they want done? The problem is easier to see if you put yourself in the position of a patient who is not pleased with the outcome of the representation. Let us assume, reasonably, that the patient discovers that court orders do not enforce themselves, and that more money must be spent on the attorney for enforcement; or, let us assume, reasonably, that the nursing home has to cut back on the number of patients in order to provide the services mandated in the order, because it cannot afford to hire the additional staff, and that our patient is one of those who has to go. Obviously, I could go on with those types of assumptions ad infinitum. Pick one that seems reasonable and, from that perspective, look back on what happened at the initiation of the relationship between the clients and the lawyer. What was decided for the clients rather than by them? Who provided the information to the clients and, although he did not mislead, is there reason to question his interest? What kind of fees were charged, and who decided that? What did the fees cover? Was the attorney hired to pursue a judgment or to solve a problem? Should I go on?

No, I see the point, but what they got was better than no representation at all.

Yes, it was, but that was not the alternative. Our professional ideal of meaningful participation reaches out to these prospective clients. Our obligations as professionals extend to the nursing home residents before they become our clients, and it is an obligation to provide meaningful participation. The problem in the hypothetical is that Laura has shifted the social worker's role to being a "bird dog" for Laura.

If Laura was concerned with meaningful participation by these patients in the resolution of their dispute with the nursing home, she would describe various approaches to the problem, describe potential legal remedies, describe various ways of gaining access to the legal system and lawyers, explore various options for the patients as prospective clients, and, in essence, say: "There are good remedies through the law, and otherwise, for these patients and they will need a lawyer for that. See that they get one." If the social worker wanted to recommend Laura, that would be for him to decide.

Instead, Laura has offered one option and created a conflict of interest for the social worker which colors his decision and the advice he gives. Laura has acted this way, in her own words, because she is ruled in her actions by a personal ideal of wealth rather than a professional ideal of meaningful participation. She has elevated her own desires to the level of principles.[2] Laura uses the clients as means towards her ends. Our professional ideal insists that clients are ends, in and of themselves, and that we not treat them otherwise.

To the extent that restrictions on solicitation, and on advertising, serve the purposes of our professional ideal, they are legitimate; to the extent that they do not, they aren't.

Professor Freedman, the author of the hypothetical, as I mentioned before, often speaks of an obligation to chase ambulances and, in doing so, turns a term of reprobation on its head and forces us to reexamine its premises. By this phrase, he reminds us that what we do for people is a positive good. As a doctor rushes to the scene of an accident, so should we. But the problem addressed by the term "ambulance chaser" was never directed at something inherently wrong with the delivery of legal services. The problem it seeks to describe is the delivery of legal services with the sole motivation of the acquisition of wealth. The fear is that the ambulance chaser will use the victims as means towards his or her ends of wealth, and that the victims are overly vulnerable to that. As in the Laura Eagle hypothetical, returning to the premises makes us see, I believe, that restrictions on solicitation, rather than being in opposition to our professional obligation to make our services available are, or can be, in harmony with it by protecting what we mean by "services."

Whether the present restrictions on solicitation are in harmony with our professional obligations is a difficult question. Professor Freedman believes that the Laura Eagle hypothetical can be varied so that she is acting consistently with our profes-

---

2. The phrase is from R. Stevens, *supra* chapter 1, note 9, at 22.

sional ideal but still in violation of ethical regulations governing solicitation.[3] If so, then those regulations are simply wrong, and Professor Freedman has served as our teacher in allowing us to discover the errors of our ways once again.

In the hypothetical, Laura was said to believe in "cab rank." Is there a professional obligation to represent anyone who walks in the door? Is that what you meant by an obligation to represent unpopular clients and causes?

No and no. Even in England, where "cab rank" is the rule, it does not translate in practice into an obligation to represent anyone who walks in the door.[4] The American rule has been

---

3. Professor Freedman believes that Laura would be acting consistently with our professional ideal, and yet still in violation of solicitation rules, if, after the solicitation, and "[b]efore suing on their behalf, Laura carefully explained to the interested patients all of the potential advantages and disadvantages of a class action and of alternative courses of action that might be taken. The patients unanimously and enthusiastically decided that they wanted the class action brought on their behalf." (Correspondence from Prof. Freedman, 9/10/87 and 9/19/87.)

Prof. Freedman uses the hypothetical as a very strong attack on existing solicitation rules. I use it not to support those rules, but to articulate a standard to be applied to any solicitation rules, past, present, or future. Our purposes are different. I disagree with him, however, when he says that his change to the hypothetical eliminates all concerns with our professional ideal. Even "bait and switch" victims do not complain when the "switch" is much better than the "bait," but that does not eliminate our concerns with the tactic. The gravity of the situation facing the clients in Prof. Freedman's hypothetical tends to obscure this point. It is not enough to say, as Prof. Freedman does, that a change was in someone's real interest if he or she would acknowledge that it was after the change was made. There are too many dangers down that road. Prof. Freedman knows that better than anyone else, and, *if* I am right in this argument, it is only because his deep concern for the welfare of others has led him to an insignificant error. You can learn more about professionalism from his deep concern than you can from arguments about how best to act upon it.

4. This is true because of the limited role of barristers to whom the rule applies and because of the way in which barristers get their briefs from

that you should not lightly refuse service and you should not do so for reasons inconsistent with the professional ideal.[5] The latter is what the obligation to represent unpopular clients and causes is all about. It would be inconsistent with the ideal to refuse representation solely because a client or a cause was unpopular, and particularly inconsistent with the ideal to do that out of fear of bad publicity or public sentiment or some other self-interest concern.

The usual examples of service to the ideal are the Black lawyer representing the Klan in seeking a parade permit or the Jewish lawyer assisting the Nazis in getting permission for a political demonstration.

If you cannot refuse them, whom can you refuse? What are reasons for refusing clients consistent with the professional ideal? For example, what if the client is proposing criminal activity?

There are some obvious reasons which are consistent with the ideal, such as refusing because of workload or conflicting interests or even conflicting personalities which will make it difficult for you to provide meaningful participation. Your example, a client who proposed criminal activity, is another reason consistent with the ideal.

---

solicitors and clerks. The rule in England seems designed, primarily, to insure that the task of representing unpopular criminal defendants is spread among the barristers so that no barristers can be tainted by the representation of unpopular criminal defendants.

As discussed below, see pp. 49-53, the representation of criminal defendants—even "guilty" ones—is not an example of not refusing because of moral reasons. It is interesting to note that the English bar's advice to barristers is that it is wrong to represent a client who admits his guilt to the barrister prior to the representation. If the client admits guilt during the representation, the advice is to represent to the extent necessary to test the government's case. *See* W. Boulton, *A Guide to Conduct And Etiquette At The Bar Of England And Wales* 70-72 (6th ed. 1975).

5. *See, e.g., Model Code Of Professional Responsibility* EC 2-26 (1981).

How is that consistent with it?

It is consistent with it because the professional ideal is an ideal within a society. Your obligation to provide meaningful participation is limited to participation which is within the rules of the society. There is no professional obligation to provide participation which is outside of those rules.

One way of viewing this is simply that society does not permit people to do what the client proposes to do. Assisting in that, even if the assistance itself is not defined by the society as criminal, is wrong regardless of the apparent loss of autonomy for the client. In a sense, that autonomy was given up by living within a society.[6]

Another way of viewing it is that we are only concerned with those things that get in the way of who the client is. The laws of a society do not do that because the client *is* a person within that society and is defined by it in part. The client cannot be who he is without that society.

---

6. I know that I am in deep water in saying what I have said in the text, but I think that we can stay afloat with it. Part of the problem is that many readers are going to equate autonomy with limitless freedom, despite my prior warning, and my statement in the text does not discourage that adequately. Autonomy has no meaning in the context of limitless freedom. It requires restrictions on freedom to exist as a concept. As Bernard Williams has said, in discussing a Kantian rational agent, restrictions on what you do make it possible to be an autonomous person, "more than that, it is also a condition of being a . . . person, of living a life at all." B. Williams, *Ethics And The Limits Of Philosophy* 57 (1985). Properly understood, personal autonomy is an ideal within a society and dependent upon it. It makes good sense that our professional ideal reflects that.

As I have said in the text, *supra* at 7, autonomy is a derivative ideal. It is derived from the fact that there is unique moral value in what it means to be you. What it means to be you is a meaning within history and community.

What if the client proposes activity which is not criminal, but immoral? Are you free to refuse to represent that client?

You are free to be true to your own morality in judging the moral value of the representation, and that means that you are free to refuse to represent clients for moral reasons.

How do you square that with representing the Klan and Nazis?

The Black attorney and the Jewish attorney who represented those clients with a belief in the professional ideal, or the First Amendment, or in equality, or whatever, were not doing anything inconsistent with their own morality. It is a mistake to see them as acting inconsistently with some private moral self.[7]

Of course, those are easy cases. It is difficult, within the shared liberal values of our society, to describe a parade and a political demonstration as immoral even when they are for immoral causes.

Let's make it tougher.

I thought you'd say that.

What if the client asks the attorney to do something which is not criminal, but which the attorney cannot do and be true to his or her morality? How do you reconcile that refusal with the professional ideal?

I believe it can be reconciled with the ideal, but it is going to take me a while to get around to a straight answer to that question because the answer needs to be given in a more complete context. Part of the problem is that what I have said about proposed criminal activity does not apply to proposed

---

7. *See* Schneyder, "Moral Philosophy's Standard Misconception of Legal Ethics," 1984 *Wis. L. Rev.* 1529, 1541 (1984).

immoral activity. We know with some certainty, some *legal* certainty, that proposed criminal activity has been removed by society from the permissible range of individual autonomy. We do not know that with proposed immoral activity. Immoral conduct is condemned by society but it is not removed from individual autonomy. Accordingly, it is one thing for society to deny certain forms of participation by clients through legislative and judicial processes; it is quite another for participation to be denied by an attorney's sense of morality.

From this perspective, it looks as if the value of the attorney's personal morality must be balanced against the value of service to the professional ideal. If both of these are matters of inherent value, that is, value not derived from consequences, the balancing is going to be very difficult to do.

We will have to face this apparent difficulty eventually, but, for now, we can avoid it because I believe that there is another point which needs to be made first. We are ignoring the fact that our professional ideal requires reflecting on the ends of the representation.

You lost me. Can you give me an example of what you mean?

How about playing with another hypothetical?

Fine.

This one is an old favorite for the profession and the advice given about it has varied over time. This value-laden formulation of it is by Michael D. Bayles.

"A prospective client asks a lawyer to defend him in a suit for breach of contract. The prospective client orally agreed to pay an elderly couple two thousand dollars if they would manage the rental of his house while he was out of the country for two years. The elderly couple have completely fulfilled their part of the agreement and due to recent illnesses and financial losses need the money to pay rent and other necessities. However, the wealthy prospective client wants to defend on the Statute of Frauds barring enforcement of oral contracts which cannot be completed within a year."[8]

Assume that the Statute would apply as Professor Bayles assumes it will. You and I know that there may be quasi-contractual remedies available to the elderly couple, and that there are good ways around a Statute of Frauds defense. But, for the sake of the hypothetical, let us assume that Professor Bayles has found a situation in which the law permits something that the attorney may think is morally wrong.

Am I free to refuse to represent this client if I believe it would be immoral for me to do so?

Yes, but do not be too hasty in reaching your decision.

And you believe that refusing to represent this client is consistent with the professional ideal?

Yes, I do. Although I admit that the argument is a difficult one to make. It may be that we will need to look outside of our description of the professional ideal to justify the refusal. If we do that, the simple answers will be that the morality of your service to the professional ideal is a part of your personal morality, but not all of it,[9] and that moral obligations are only one kind of moral considerations. There are others.

But we are getting way ahead of ourselves. It may be that you will agree with me that we do not need to look outside of our description of the professional ideal to find a moral basis for refusing to represent this client.

---

8. Bayles, "A Problem of Clean Hands: Refusal to Provide Professional Services," 5 *Social Theory and Practice* 165-81 (1979) (reprinted in M. Davis and F. Elliston, eds., *Ethics And The Legal Profession* 428-40 [1986]).

9. *See generally* Shaffer, "The Legal Ethics of The Two Kingdoms," 17 *Val. U.L. Rev.* 3 (1983).

Isn't this sort of silly? Even if I refuse to represent this client someone else will, and it will all end the same.

No, it is not. Someone else is not you.[10] The question is whether or not your refusal is consistent with your professionalism, your obligation of service to the professional ideal.

The obligation is a personal one. It is you who are called upon to provide meaningful participation and, if you do not, you cannot reconcile your actions with your obligation by saying that someone else did it for you. In this sense, as far as professionalism is concerned, you are always the last lawyer in town.

Maybe we ought to get back to the hypothetical.

I agree. Let's look at what is happening in it with more care. The moral wrong here is in not fulfilling the agreed upon contractual obligation. In the hypothetical, the Statute of Frauds is seen as a means to that immoral end, but there is nothing immoral in the Statute of Frauds as a means. The Statute is not an obviously unjust or immoral law. It is not a mere technicality.[11] As you know, or will find out soon, it has some rather clear social purposes, albeit prudential ones. If you refuse to assert the Statute in this hypothetical, you are circumventing both legislative and judicial processes in regards to the Statute's purposes.

If we forget about the underlying moral obligation to fulfill the agreement for the moment, the effect of your representation is to assist this client in keeping this dispute free from social interference and social coercion, in other words, keeping it out of the legal system. Your representation permits the client to say that this dispute is a moral one between the parties and, through the operation of the Statute, that society agrees with that.

---

10. The refusal-to-represent issue is debated at length in M. Davis and F. Elliston, eds., *Ethics And The Legal Profession* 428-64 (1986).

11. M. Bayles, *supra* note 8, at 428.

Of course, it would be pure sophistry for an attorney to separate means from ends in this way to avoid the moral issue. We cannot engage in such sophistry, even if we wanted to, because of the nature of the representation required by our professional ideal.

What do you mean?

Go back to the problem-solving and decision-making processes. The problem-solving processes tell us to ask the client, after explaining how we could use the Statute of Frauds to avoid social enforcement of the legal obligation, about the remaining moral obligation.

Why?

Simply stated, because his morality is part of who he is, and he is the one who is to participate in this dispute. The moral outcome of it is his moral outcome.

But hasn't he already stated his position on that? Isn't it implicit in his coming to you?

You are back to the client who walks in the door asking for a bankruptcy, aren't you? This is what I meant before when I said that we were forgetting about "reflecting on the ends of the representation." Moral decisions are not just gut reactions.[12] They can be benefited by systematic thought processes just like any other decisions, the decision to file for bankruptcy, for example.

This is different.

How?

---

12. *See* D. Campbell, *supra* chapter 1, note 3, at 62.

By raising morality you are really imposing your own morality on the client. That is a very easy way out of the issue of the client who proposes immoral activity, and it is inconsistent with your professional ideal because it is you who is really participating, not the client.

If I impose morality by raising it, then you are right. I do not believe I do. We are back to the same concerns you had before about reflecting on the ends of the representation. Is an assumption of willingness to talk to others and to submit one's moral judgment to friendly scrutiny somehow inconsistent with moral autonomy?[13] That way of thinking about morals is, I believe, another example of attempting to fix the client into one unambiguous entity and, in the process, to destroy the real client's participation in the dispute. Your client knows who she is, but she can't know who she will be. If I am really trying to treat the client as a human being defining herself in the dispute, then that includes morality. To exclude it is to deny the client the opportunity to become who she is in the dispute. In other words, I believe that I need to raise morality in order to do a good job in accordance with the professional ideal.

There is no doubt that by raising morality—the "character of the act"—I am changing my client. I am, in that sense, participating. But change is not distortion. Who my client is includes processes of change. The status quo of my client is not static. As long as I act honestly to avoid manipulation, my client remains the true participant to the extent that anyone can in a relationship with another. In fact, the manner in which you approach problems as a man or woman of practical reason is likely to bring about changes in your clients. There is nothing wrong with that if the goal remains meaningful participation by the client and if the harmony of action and feeling which practical reason seeks to produce remains your client's harmony.

---

13. *See* J. Raz, *supra* chapter 1, note 9.

There is another side to this question of raising morality. At times, you and your client will go beyond your respective roles in the relationship and form a friendship in which your client can best be who he is.[14] That type of a relationship with clients is one in which you can come close to accomplishing the ideal of meaningful participation. I do not think that you would question raising morality with a friend or view that as imposing your morality upon another.

But it is presumptuous of me as a lawyer to ask questions about morality to a client who has not become a friend! I should stick with the law.

Look, there is absolutely no doubt that all of this can be done in a very off-putting way, if that is your concern. There is also no doubt that there is a great risk of attorney dominance in client-attorney conversations. But I do not believe that raising morality is necessarily presumptuous or domineering. In fact, I believe that it is presumptuous not to.

How?

There is no such thing as "sticking with the law." There is no such thing as pure legal advice. What appears as such always makes assumptions about the other aspects of the problem and about what the client wants. It is presumptuous to think that you know the client that well or that the client is like some general conception you have of clients and of what they want.

One other point—I think that you are ignoring that *not* raising morality shapes the client's morality. You cannot avoid the moral issue. It is like politics in that regard. *Not* to be political is one form of being political. *Not* to raise morality is one way of making a moral statement. I know that you are

---

14. *See generally* Shaffer, "The Ethics of Dissent and Friendship in the Americans Professions," 88 *W. Va. L. Rev.* 623 (1986).

concerned about paternalism, as you have said before, and I imagine that you are concerned about that here, but there are many ways of being a father to someone. Some are good and some are bad. The bad ones here are those ways of fathering which destroy who the other person is, in the process of trying to help, by denying to that person the opportunity to participate for himself in the dispute. There is a difference in serving someone and in helping someone. Beyond that, I think, we can go back once again to our assumptions about our clients (i.e., that they know what they want, they intend to get it, and they are willing to discuss it,) to assure us that we are not overstepping the bounds of respectful conversation.

O.K. But even if being a professional means raising the moral obligation with the client, how likely is it that it will make any difference? You have not resolved the issue yet.

No, I have not, and I do not know what the likelihood is that raising morality will make any difference. It depends on the morality of our clients. I do know, however, that the processes we go through with our clients are moral processes and that, whatever the likelihood is, it is greater than it would be without going through those processes because all of our clients have some morality.

How are they moral processes?

You provide a distance which permits recognition of the dispute as a moral event. In raising morality as part of the process of solving the problem, you create the "stop and think" of moral reasoning. In trying out various definitions of the problem and alternative solutions, and in evaluating those, your client tests her beliefs and values by seeing what they mean within the dispute. In trying to show your client how to convert her position to a shared one, in order to persuade others, your client considers others and society and, in essence, listens to the voices of others and society in making decisions about the dispute.[15]

As others have noted, the processes of legal problem solving and legal analysis closely resemble those of moral reasoning.[16]

You asked me near the beginning about the social value of the professional ideal. The cumulative effect of thinking about disputes in this way is an important benefit to society. The same caveat I gave then applies now, however. It is very easy for a service to individuals to become in reality a service to social ends and not really a service to the individual at all. The irony is that when that happens it destroys what was benefiting the society to begin with.

That is still very abstract, but let it go for now. I want to come back to the hypothetical but, before we do that, it looks to me that the nature of the relationship between the lawyer and the client is central to your conception of serving the professional ideal of meaningful participation. The relationship is a rather delicate one, isn't it?

Yes, it is, and the professional ideal requires a lot of protection for the relationship. The obligations of confidentiality and the avoidance of conflicting interests, which I mentioned back in the beginning, are both a part of the protection required by the professional ideal. The obligation to avoid conflicting interests says that nothing else, other than the client, is to participate through you in the client's dispute. The obligation of confidentiality says that the client will determine when, where, and how she will be presented to others through you. This is the essence of participation. You will study the contours of these obligations in detail in your law school course in legal ethics or you have already done so. For me, the key to both

---

15. "Participation," *supra* chapter 1, note 6, at ____ .

16. *See, e.g.*, T. Perry, *Moral Reasoning And Truth: An Essay In Philosophy & Jurisprudence* (1976); S. Stoljar, *Moral And Legal Reasoning* (1980).

obligations is to read them in light of the ideal and to understand the role of consent by the client.

Does consent by the client mean that it is permissible to violate my professional obligation?

No, when the client consents there is no violation. Conflicts of interest and disclosures of confidential information are not inherently wrong nor do they *necessarily* produce bad consequences. They are wrong because they are in violation of the relationship with the client. When there is consent by the client, there is no violation of the relationship. The profession has limited client consent to some conflicts of interests in situations where we are afraid that meaningful participation by the client in the consent decision was unlikely or when meaningful participation by the client does not seem possible given the conflict of interests. Again, these are subjects for your course work.

Well then, let's get back to the Statute of Frauds hypothetical. You still have not answered the question about reconciling the refusal to represent that client with the professional ideal.

This is going to put you off a bit, but before going back to it I would like to introduce yet another hypothetical. This one involves immoral means to moral ends—in contrast with the Statute of Fraud hypothetical. Once again we are in the debt of the provocative Professor Freedman.

"Two experienced and conscientious lawyers (A and B) once asked me to help them to resolve an ethical problem. They represented a party for whom they were negotiating a complex contract involving voluminous legal documents. The attorneys on the other side were insistent upon eliminating a particular guarantee provision, and A and B had been authorized by their client to forego the guarantee. The other lawyers had overlooked, however, that the same guarantee appeared elsewhere in the documents where it was more broadly and unambiguously stated. Having agreed to eliminate the guarantee provision, with specific reference to a particular clause on a particular page, were A and B obligated to call the attention of opposing counsel to the similar clause on a different page?"[17]

O.K. What should the lawyer do?

I hope you see that the first step is to talk to the client about all of this and that in talking to the client the lawyer raises the moral issue.

It still seems presumptuous to me. I do not have any special moral expertise. Why do lawyers have any claims of special knowledge or special abilities regarding morality?

As people, we do not; as lawyers with clients, we do. As I said before, we create a distance from the dispute which permits recognition of it as a moral event. Also, we become accustomed to thinking through disputes in this way.[18] Our ideal of meaningful participation tells us that participation includes participation by the moral self, so we go looking for it.

I do not think the problem of being off-putting, or of lacking special knowledge or special abilities, is much of a problem in this hypothetical because it seems to me that much of the moral reasoning required here is the same as the required practical reasoning. Practical reasoning is what lawyers do

---

17. *See* Freedman, "The Lawyer as a Hired Gun," adapted from Freedman, "Professional Responsibility in a Professional System," 27 *Cath. U.L. Rev.* 1971 (1978) (reprinted in A. Gerson, *Lawyers' Ethics: Contemporary Dilemmas* 63-71 [1980]).

18. I believe that there is a form of morality inherent in the way we think through disputes with our clients. *See* "Participation," *supra* chapter 1, note 6, at _____ . In essence, we provide the reflection and the detachment of the Kantian rational agent in those conversations. *See* B. Williams, *supra* note 6, at 54-70.

best. I do not want to claim too much here, but I think you will find that moral reasoning is often practical reasoning.

Isn't there a real risk that what is happening here is not meaningful participation at all, but that lawyers are serving a social purpose of keeping people in check and not really serving the individual?

Yes, there is, and the image of lawyers as cops is an attractive one to lots of different people. I hope that is not what I have described to you.

No, it is not, but the effect might very well be the same.

It may be, but how you get to that effect is everything. There is a very long history of sociologists and historians describing lawyers as serving the function of a buffer between the individual and society.[19] If that is done by lawyers imposing social values upon their clients, then it is inconsistent with our professional ideal. But if the buffering arises from service to the professional ideal, that is, from providing meaningful participation, then the buffering is just a reflection of who our clients are. The society lives within the individual as the individual lives within the society.[20] Buffering can be no more than this truth showing itself in thousands of client-lawyer relationships. Others have described lawyers as providing a buffer not between the individual and society, but between individuals. They describe lawyers as peacemakers.[21] The same objection applies. If that peace is just a reflection of who our

---

19. *See, e.g.*, T. Parsons, *Essays In Sociological Theory*, "A Sociologist Looks at the Legal Profession," 384 (1954) (cited in G. Hazard and D. Rhodes, *The Legal Profession: Responsibility And Regulation* 3 n. 4 [1985]).

20. *See* Dewey's description of the individual in J. Lovinlock, *John Dewey's Philosophy Of Value* 98-123 (1972); *see generally* J. Dewey, *Theory Of The Moral Life* (1960).

21. *See, e.g.*, Burger "Isn't There A Better Way?" Annual Report on the State of the Judiciary (Jan. 24, 1982).

clients are, then we are peacemakers. If not, we are enforcers of the peace. Lawyers are not cops, but they do talk to the cop inside of each of us.[22]

But what if the cop isn't on the job? Are there no limits to what the client can do through the attorney other than the cop outside (the criminal law) and the one inside?

Yes, there are. The moral justification of what I do for my client as an attorney is dependent on the morality of my service to the professional ideal. I have no professional obligation to do anything which is not in service to that ideal, and I have a professional obligation to avoid doing things which are a disservice to it. That is the limit I impose upon my client as a professional.

But the ideal is meaningful participation by this client. That is not a limit at all.

The ideal is to provide meaningful participation to people.

What's the difference?

The difference is that, while I am under no obligation to provide meaningful participation to others in a dispute, once I have accepted a client, I cannot deny it to others consistently with the professional ideal.

I think I understand, but it is abstract. Can you give examples?

Well, for one example, meaningful participation as a professional ideal requires that I be honest with the others involved in the dispute. I cannot lie to them because to do so would deny to them the participation they are entitled to. This is true even if lying is something my client wishes me to do.

---

22. The expression is from J. Pike, *Beyond The Law* 79 (1963).

How does lying deny meaningful participation?

"In duping another by lying to him, you deprive him of the opportunity of exercising his judgment. . . . "[23] In other words, by lying you are using the other person without his knowledge. You control his participation by creating a false context for it.

Another example?

O.K., but this time in the form of yet another hypothetical. This hypothetical has been around a long time. Suppose one attorney knows that another has a drinking problem and, while the other attorney does not drink at the office, he is quite desperate for one around six o'clock. Should the attorney time a phone call offer of a settlement for the purpose of taking advantage of that weakness for his client?

Calling at six for the purpose described is a way of denying meaningful participation to that lawyer's client. You cannot do that, even if your client wants you to, consistent with your obligation of service to the professional ideal.

But lawyers do things like that all the time!

Do they? At least one researcher,[24] and there is a paucity of research on subjects like this, has found that lawyers do not act that way in communities where lawyers know each other. I do not think that means just lawyers in small towns. I think it means in legal communities. Lawyers who do a lot of bankruptcy work, for example, can form a legal community even in a very large city.

There are lawyers who believe that they have some sort of professional obligation to act like that. They call it "playing

---

23. A. Donnagan, *The Theory Of Morality* 89 (1977).

24. *See* Landon, "Clients, Colleagues, and Community: The Shaping of Zealous Advocacy in County Law Practice," 1985 *A.B.F. Res.* 81 (1985). He draws very different conclusions from his research than I do. See comments on his prior study of the same topic in Mindes, "Defining Professionalism in the Bar: Comments on Landon's Article," 1982 *A.B.F. Res. J.* 1163 (1982).

hard ball." Not only is there no such obligation, but there is a professional obligation not to act like that.

I see that you have side-tracked me into talking about the actual rather than the ideal. Do not forget that we are still talking about a professional ideal—an aspiration.

Since I got you started, one more question along the same lines. If others use techniques like calling the attorney at six, and I do not, won't my clients be at a competitive disadvantage?

Yes, and that is why it is so important not to do it.

I do not follow you.

By doing it you are offering a reason for others to join in.

At the level of principle, competitive disadvantage does not make it right to act unprofessionally. As has been said before, in the same context: "An equal right to do a wrong is contradictory."[25]

At the level of practicality, it is the nature of our professional ideal that everybody is better off, including our clients, if no one acts inconsistently with it.

I would like to get back to our Statute of Frauds hypothetical.

I thought you would say that. In my initial conversation with that prospective client, I am going to explain the Statute of Frauds, offer my prediction as to how it would be applied to his situation, and raise the subject of his moral obligation to the other party in the dispute. A lot can happen during that conversation, but, if my client insists on pursuing an end which seems to me to be immoral, I need to make a decision about the morality of my representing this client in the pursuit of

---

25. A. Goldman, *supra* chapter 1, note 1, at 272.

that end. In doing so, I am making a personal moral judgment about the moral value of the professional ideal in the context of representing this client.

So we are back to your personal morality taking precedence over the morality of the professional ideal! I thought you said you did not need that, and that refusing a client for moral reasons was consistent with the professional ideal?

That is not what I am trying to say. The professional ideal is a moral one, but *no* moral ideal, even when consistently applied, can be counted on to produce moral results all of the time. There must be an assumption behind the ideal that it will be applied in a moral fashion just as there is an assumption that it will be applied logically—and, accordingly, our professional ideal must be subject to the moral judgments of the attorney applying it.

That is not the same as the attorney's morals being in conflict with the client's, nor is it the same as the professional ideal being in conflict with the attorney's personal morality.

In other words, the attorney may have to judge the morality of serving the professional ideal in this particular case. Even if the attorney's judgment is that it would be immoral to do so, all things considered, the attorney has not acted inconsistently with the professional ideal because the ideal must assume that the attorney will make that kind of judgment. It cannot be a moral ideal in any other way.

That looks like fancy footwork to me.

It may be. If nothing else, I hope that it will clarify your analysis of the Statute of Frauds hypothetical. Part of what I am trying to show here is that the lawyer's moral judgments can benefit from systematic thought processes as much as the client's can. Of course, there are limits to the thought processes we are using. Trying to explicate a professional ideal fully, without a resort to judgment at some point, would end in pedantry. I believe that a resort to personal judgment is required in any conception of professionalism. I can view that resort to personal judgment as inconsistent with the professional ideal, as you would have me do, or I can view it as consistent with it. If I am right that the resort to personal judgment will always be required, why not view that as consistent with the ideal in the same way that other requirements of thought, such as logic, are consistent with it?

So what is your decision about the Statute of Frauds hypothetical?

I don't know. I haven't had the conversation with the client. You and I can imagine how the conversation might go, and we can explore the ramifications of different conversations to prepare ourselves for them. But the answer has to be discovered in the real process.[26]

I know this answer does not please you. It does not please most law students or most lawyers. It may make you feel better to recognize that the legal profession is not alone in this struggle. All professions assume in their professional ideals that it is good to serve all people. When someone proves that it isn't, it causes trouble for the professional ideal. We may have it worse than others because of the nature of the service we provide. We are much more involved with people than the other professions are.

I am happy, for now, with my own resolution of this issue. It works for me. It may for you. So that you will know my bias, I should tell you that I have very seldom found it necessary to refuse to represent a client for moral reasons, and it is equally seldom that I have had moral regrets for having represented a client.

---

26. *See* B. Williams, *supra* note 6, for a general discussion of finding answers in the process and the limits of ethical theory.

What about the second guarantee clause hypothetical?

Much of what has already been said applies. This may be characterized as an act of dishonesty which denies meaningful participation to the other party and, if that characterization fits, I have a professional obligation to avoid the act.[27] Under the particular circumstances, however, the characterization of dishonesty may not fit well. I am afraid that the truth is in the details once again. Our professional ideal does not apply itself. We have to apply it.

The decision here may be complex because in judging the morality of your representation you must take into consideration the relationship you have formed with your client. For example, what are his expectations and what role did you play in creating them?

It is far too easy to forget about that relationship in making moral judgments because we have developed the habit of thinking only about outcomes. Back in the Statute of Frauds hypothetical, for example, even if I refuse to represent that client, I do not know if I have prevented the harm to the elderly couple. The prevention of that harm depends upon chance events and circumstances more than it does on my decision. My decision has to be based not on outcome, but on the character of my act, and the character of my act, in that situation, is shaped, primarily, by the way I am treating my client and the way he is treating me.

It seems to me that lurking behind your conception of professionalism is some notion that a lot of the problems you are discussing will go away when you raise them directly with your clients.

You may be right.

---

27. The A.B.A. Standing Committee on Ethics and Professional Responsibility has offered its guidance for a similar situation in an informal opinion. *See* A.B.A. Committee on Ethics and Professional Responsibility, Informal Opinion 1581 (1986).

Isn't that putting an awful lot of trust in people?

Well, it is not necessary to my conception that they always go away, but, to answer the question, yes, it is putting a lot of trust in people or in something through people. From my perspective, I do not see that there is any other choice.

What happens then if the client is an incompetent?

The professional ideal gives us a direction to follow, but not much specific guidance on how to follow it. The direction is obvious: Treat incompetent clients as if they were competent to the fullest extent possible. In other words, you try as best you can to maintain a normal client-lawyer relationship so that the client can participate through you.[28]

The problem of the incompetent client calls into question the core value of autonomy. It is the situation in which the term "meaningful participation" begins to lose its meaning.

As an aside, in this situation and in others, you will hear it said that lawyers should make some decisions in the client's "best interests." That phrase is a very unfortunate one. No one can possibly know what is in another person's best interests, and even if they could, that is not what is of moral value in the representation. As I said before, our clients are "ends," in and of themselves, and it is part of our task to treat them as such. It is not our task to secure for clients the benefits which result from being treated as ends by others. Confusion about that permeates throughout "best interest" talk about clients and even "individual rights" talk about clients. The problem of the incompetent client is not that he will make stupid choices—choices not in his "best interest"—but that he can make no real choice at all.

---

28. *See* Shaffer, "Advocacy as Moral Discourse," 57 *N.C.L. Rev.* 647 (1979).

Wait! Are you saying that clients have to make all of the decisions?

No, of course not, but the norm of the relationship must be client decision-making.[29] If the relationship has formed as it should, the lawyer will develop a sense of which decisions are of sufficient import to the client to require the client's attention.

Let me give you an example. In most situations, a reasonable request for a postponement is something the lawyer can decide without consulting the client. In fact, it can be a denial of meaningful participation to others in the dispute to refuse such a request in some circumstances. On the other hand, the determination of the reasonableness of the request may depend upon the client's particular circumstances and even upon the client's values. If the determination is something you judge to be of importance to the client, you should go back to him or to her with the decision. Whether to go to the client or not is your decision initially, but you make it subject to your client's scrutiny.

---

29. The issues of client-lawyer decision making are the quickest route into the central issues of professionalism. For an article defending my assertion see Strauss, "Towards A Revised Model of Attorney-Client Relationship: The Argument for Autonomy," 65 *N.C.L. Rev.* 315 (1987). *See also* Spiegal, "Lawyering and Client Decision-Making: Informed Consent and The Legal Profession," 128 *U. Pa. L. Rev.* 41 (1979) and Spiegal, "The Model Rules of Professional Conduct: Lawyer-Client Decision Making and the Role of Rules in Structuring the Lawyer-Client Dialogue," 1981 *A.B.F. Res. J.* 1003 (1980). For a fascinating debate which will show you how decision-making issues become central to all issues of professionalism, see Shaffer, "Legal Ethics and The Good Client," 36 *Cath. U.L. Rev.* 319 (1987), and Freedman, "Legal Ethics and The Suffering Client," 36 *Cath. U.L. Rev.* 331 (1987).

· THREE ·

PERSONAL MATTERS

It looks to me that your conception of professionalism sees the relationship between the client and the lawyer as a very personal one. Do not most clients come to lawyers with business matters and, if so, can you view those relationships in the same way?

It has been my experience that the relationship between business executives and their lawyers are some of the most personal client-lawyer relationships. There is often a very clear recognition on both sides that there is something more to the relationship than the fulfilling of contractual obligations. But, that aside, I understand the difficulty you are having. We tend to think of business as a single-minded pursuit. It is the equivalent of having the ends of the representation fixed in advance, when you think about it that way, and, when you do, you eliminate the cop inside.[1] In other words, it seems as if you are no longer representing people.

I am sure that you can anticipate my argument that this is a misconception, and that all I have said about reflecting on

---

1. As one professor of business ethics, Thomas Mulligan, puts it: "Success in business is not simply to maximize profit. Otherwise, we'd consider the Mafia an example of an extremely successful business." Quoted in Bliwise, "Towards A Corporate Conscience," *Duke Perspectives* 6 (1987). The image we have of the unfailingly aggressive corporate client is simply wrong.

the ends of the representation applies to business clients as well.

Yes, but I have a hard time seeing it as a misconception in the case of an attorney representing a corporation who speaks to people only in their capacity as officers of the corporation.

It is difficult for me, too, and the problem is one of substantial proportions. If you expand your description to include all lawyers working within organization, adding government lawyers and others by doing so, you are talking about two-thirds of the legal profession.[2]

There are those who say that this reality of practice differs so from the assumed norm of representing individuals, with whom you are in direct communication, in the resolution or prevention of disputes, that it challenges the basic premises of our professional ideal.[3] I think, however, that the differences are all of degree. If they are, then the challenge is not to the validity of the basic premises, but to whether the professional ideal is sufficiently realistic to serve as an ideal, as we have wondered before. The professional ideal is not descriptive. It seeks to change; not to interpret.

For me, the lawyer in the organization is in the same posture as one who has accepted representation of a particular client. Neither of these lawyers is an independent moral agent free from organizational constraints. Both must make decisions about the representation within the context of obligations and responsibilities to the client. The fact that in one case the client is a person and, in the other, an entity, does not change that. It does mean, however, that the organizational obligations and responsibilities in the latter case are much more imposing, and that the exercise of moral judgment, in the way called for

---

2. Rhodes, "Ethical Perspectives on Legal Practice," 37 *Stan. L. Rev.* 589, 590 (1985).

3. *Id.* at 591.

by our professional ideal of meaningful participation, may come with a higher price tag. That is a difference of degree and not a challenge to premises.

I do not want to downplay the problem. The questions about individual responsibilities within organizations are enormously difficult. They are questions which you have or you will encounter in almost every law school course you take. The "banality of evil"[4]—by which I mean that most evil is done by those who are not monsters, but who forget to stop and think about what they are doing—shows itself with much force within organizations because it is so difficult for individuals in organizations to stop and think. But the enormity of that problem does not mean that it is a different problem than the one faced by the "independent" lawyer with individuals for clients. It is a matter of degree.

It is, of course, much more difficult for lawyers within organizations to provide the distance needed to recognize disputes as moral events. Again, it is a matter of degree, and some of the distance, as I implied before, will always be there in the processes of legal reasoning and in the consideration of shared social norms. All of the difficulties of finding the cop within the corporation only increase the value of one who must do so in order to do a good job.

Basically, if you agreed with my answer to your last question, that is, that it is a misconception to view business as having unambiguous and fixed ends, and that we are really representing people even when the client is a corporation, then all else I have said seems to me to follow naturally. That is easy to see if you view corporations as people acting as "we's," just as we view other organizations from the family to the government.[5]

---

4. H. Arendt, *The Life Of The Mind* 3 (1971); *see also* H. Arendt, *Eichmann in Jerusalem* (1963).

5. *See* Shaffer, "The Legal Ethics of Radical Individualism," 65 *Tex. L. Rev.* 963 (1987) for an understanding of the need to represent "we's."

By the way, the government lawyer has an easier task, *conceptually*. Her client always wants her to use means and to seek ends which are within the shared legal and moral norms of our society, consistent with our founding myth of the rule of law, and protective of our democratic processes. (I use the word "myth" with great respect.)

"Conceptually" is italicized because there are enormous pressures on government lawyers, particularly prosecutors, to be winners rather than lawyers. The pressures are so strong that I often wonder if we are asking too much of our prosecutors. But now I am asking the question you usually ask. Is our ideal realistic enough as an ideal?

If you do not mind, I would like to leave the client side of the client-lawyer relationship and talk more about the lawyer's. Back in the beginning you said that the professional ideal must be something other than just a benefit to the professional, and I have noticed how often the obligations of professionalism seem to run counter to the self-interests, particularly the financial self-interests, of the lawyer. It looks like much of professionalism is a willing denial of self-interest in service to the professional ideal.

I think it is confusing to state it that way. If you do, you will inevitably hear the response that you cannot be a real person in your job if you are constantly denying yourself. That response is usually part of a plea for non-professional representation. I think our professional ideal requires us to see our self-interest in service to the professional ideal.

What do you mean by that?

Service to the professional ideal, professionalism in other words, is one way of self-fulfillment.[6] Perhaps the best way of

---

6. *See* Richards, "Moral Theory, The Developmental Psychology of Ethical Autonomy and Professionalism," 31 *J. Legal Educ.* 359, 361 (1981).

describing that is to go back to the original meaning of "profession" and to describe the true professional as a person under a calling.[7] Being under a calling does require self-discipline, but not a denial of self-interests. In fact, I think it is fair to say that self-discipline is a central attribute of all professionalism.[8]

On a more mundane level, there is absolutely no doubt, as your question asserts, that the obligation of professionalism means moving away from a personal ideal of wealth.[9] Ours is a service profession and one who cannot find self-fulfillment in service to others is in the wrong job.

Doesn't all of this talk of professionalism boil down to being a moral person when deciding whom to represent and how to represent them?

Yes, I think you can say that, if you recognize that consideration of the moral value of your calling is part of what you mean by being a moral person. Lawyer morality is ordinary morality which takes into consideration the moral value of professional obligations. That is not very difficult for most of us to do because the morality of our professional obligations are not unique. They are, instead, the central values of our society.[10]

Our morality is no more than: Be moral, all things considered. Ordinary morality is the same. It is easy to get confused

---

7. *See* J. Pike, *supra* chapter 2, note 22, at 65-66. For the history of the term, *see* D. Campbell, *supra* chapter 1, note 3, at 80.

8. D. Campbell, *supra* chapter 1, note 3, at 100.

9. Our failure to do that is one primary cause of what is perceived as a crisis of professionalism. *See* " '.... In The Spirit of Public Service:' A Blueprint For The Rekindling Of Lawyer Professionalism," *American Bar Association Commission On Professionalism* 50 (1986). The most frequent comment made by practicing attorneys who reviewed earlier drafts of this book was that the greatest enemy of professionalism is the single minded pursuit of personal wealth.

10. *See* J. Pike, *supra* chapter 2, note 22, at 26 and Schneyder, *supra* chapter 2, note 7, at 1557.

about that because we tend to look only at the effect legal representation can have on others and ask if an abstract moral agent, free to choose without consideration of relationships and obligations, would desire that effect. People who look at us that way usually say that our morality is a role morality which is different from ordinary morality. Another version of the same thing is to say that lawyers must be different moral people at the office than they are at home. That is ironic. The only thing that remains constant between the office and the home is who the lawyer is as a person, his or her character, integrity, virtues, values, and so forth. The lawyer brings all of who she is to the moral judgments she makes in both places. She *must* decide from who she is.[11]

I think personal morality includes consideration of relationships and obligations. In other words, personal morality is role morality and cannot be the morality of an abstract, free-floating, moral agent. Of course, roles are never completely clear and, even if they were, the role would not "unfailingly produce particular courses of actions."[12] I hope you have seen that in our discussions.

But I fear that I am preaching now. I have a tendency to do that. Am I losing my audience?

Well, maybe. It is clear to me that you hold the legal profession in very high regard.

I hold our ideal in very high regard.

I am not sure that I can feel as good as you do about service to that ideal. There are parts of the practice of law that bother me quite a bit.

For example?

---

11. The phrase is Williams'. *See* B. Williams, *supra* chapter 2, note 6, at 200.

12. A. MacIntyre, *After Virtue* 169, 209 (1981) (cited in Schneyder, *supra* chapter 2, note 7, at 1536).

Well, I am almost embarrassed to ask it because it is a cliché question. How can I try to convince a jury or a judge that a criminal defendant is innocent when I know that he is guilty? How can I do that and still think of myself as doing something of moral value?

You are assuming that there is no question as to his guilt?

Yes.

O.K. I hope that question is not a cliché. It is certainly not an easy one to answer. On the whole, lawyers, even criminal defense lawyers, do not do a very good job of providing good answers to it. In fact, I am constantly reminded in conversations that there are many lawyers who believe that there are no good answers to that question, and that it is morally wrong to defend a client you know to be guilty and wrong to present a "false defense,"[13] one which questions a known truth.

Before we get to the substance of this, I should tell you that each criminal defense lawyer has to answer this question individually. Some find the answer in religion and see clearly the need for mercy.[14] Others find the answer in cynicism. They believe that nothing good can ever come out of a criminal conviction. In other words, they believe that our system of criminal justice is so inherently flawed that the right thing to do under any circumstance is to fight the criminal conviction. It does not matter at all that the defendant happens to be guilty.

I offer the latter to you for whatever consideration you wish to give it. I promise you that it will hold an attraction for you

---

13. *See* Subin, "The Criminal Lawyer's Differing Mission: Reflections on the 'Right' to Present a False Defense," 1 *Geo. J. Legal Ethics* 125 (1987).

14. For a very moving description of one lawyer's conversion to that position see F. Gedicks, "Justice or Mercy" (unpublished manuscript on file with author) (1987). F. Gedicks is an Assistant Professor at Mercer Law School.

if you become a criminal defense lawyer. That justification does not work for me.

What does?

Well, I am afraid that you are going to be disappointed because it is the usual justification of putting the government's case to the test.

You mean protecting individual rights?

Yes and no. The goal of representation is client participation and, in criminal defense work, that almost always means seeking the client's freedom. The goal is not the protection of the client's rights. There is no doubt, however, that one of the effects of criminal defense representation is the protection of individual rights.

When most people talk about protecting rights they tend to forget that there are two kinds of freedom. Much of "rights" talk is about freedom from something, but there is also "freedom to."[15] In fact, much of meaningful participation is a "freedom to" concern. If you mean both when you say "rights," then we may be saying the same thing.

I see putting the government's case to the test as a way of keeping the individual free to participate in the dispute with the government. It is difficult for me to see how it can ever be morally wrong for a criminal defendant to have a say in the dispute or wrong for the lawyer to make that say possible.

But the form the "say," the participation, takes is dishonesty. What the guilty criminal defendant is saying in the situation in my question is a lie.

It looks like it.

---

15. The expression is from E. Fromm, *Escape From Freedom* 35 (1941). Kant's description of 'positive and negative' freedoms is a similar conception.

What do you mean?

For example, if two brothers are playing and something gets broken, it would be a lie for one of them to help the guilty brother by saying to the parent that his brother did not do it when he knows he did. It would also be dishonest to dispute with the parent whether or not what he knows happened really did.

It is easy to view the lawyer representing a guilty criminal defendant as doing exactly the same thing. But the lawyer is not. The situation is not the same because our society does not want to treat the individual's relationship with the government the same as the relationship between a parent and a child. Our society tries to shape the relationship between an individual and the government into a relationship it likes, in part, by requiring the government to justify to others, in all cases, the harm it intends to do to any individual. In this society, because we are very concerned with this relationship, we say that the justification must be based on facts which are proved by the government beyond a reasonable doubt.

What all of that means in the situation of a criminal trial is that there is only one truth which concerns us, and that is the truth of the government's case. No other truth matters. We permit the defendant the dishonesty of the not guilty plea, and of the questioning of what he knows to be the truth, and, in doing so, we destroy the dishonesty of the plea and of the questioning. The same would be true if the parent defined the relationship with the children that way. That is so because dishonesty is both personal and social. It is not dishonest to lie to others when society removes the expectation of the truth for its own moral purposes.

Of course, when the criminal defendant creates an expectation of honesty in others—when he is testifying under oath or offering as true the testimony of others—the obligation of honesty is still there. But when he lies, or you lie for him, to put the government to the test by a plea of not guilty or a questioning of what he knows to be the truth, that is not lying at all because only one truth matters—the truth of the government's case.

We make it difficult for people to understand this by describing the trial as a search for truth and justice. The criminal trial is not a search for truth. It is a search for the truth of the government's case. That is what the burden of proof, the requirement that we impose upon our government of justifying the harm it intends to do to any individual, means.

How can it be wrong for lawyers to make it possible for criminal defendants to participate in his or her dispute with the government when it is understood that defense by a guilty defendant is not dishonest if we believe that the government should justify the harm it intends to do to him or her? The usual way of saying all of this is that the guilty criminal defendant in our society is always entitled to participate as if he were innocent.

All of what I have said about representing guilty criminal defendants is an example of the type of moral judgment I was talking about in the Statute of Frauds hypothetical. In fact, there are many similarities here. My judgment, in the abstract, is that it is almost always moral for me to serve our professional ideal in the representation of a guilty criminal defendant. That is the type of moral judgment about applying the ideal that the ideal must assume I will make.

But why shouldn't the criminal defendant admit his guilt?

If you mean isn't that the honorable thing to do, I think it is. The question here is the morality of your representation of the criminal defendant if he does not do the honorable thing.

But there is a chance that the criminal defendant will harm others and that you will have helped him do that.

There is that chance. I have helped him retain his freedom when the government could not justify taking it from him on its own terms. How he uses his freedom must be his decision. Your question is about the price of freedom and of the type of relationship there should be between the government and the individual. The fact that the answers our society gives now to that question come with a price tag attached does not make it morally wrong to represent guilty criminal defendants.

I do not mean that lawyers are unconcerned with what their client may do in the future. You see evidence of that concern constantly in all that lawyers do for some criminal defense clients in trying to help them be the person they would like to be. The first step in that is treating the criminal defendant as a person by telling him through your actions that there is a unique moral value in what it means to be "him." You may be surprised at the results, as others have been before you. Why give to the genuinely evil the power to control your thinking about people, including them?

And I suppose you see no harm in a criminal defense attorney cross-examining a witness he knows is telling the truth?

Of course I see the harm. I think, however, that it can be done with moral justification in many cases. The choice is a tragic one, but so are most difficult moral choices. The cross-examinations test the reliability of the facts of the government cases because, *as a matter of principle*, the government cannot justify the harm it intends to do on unreliable facts—even those which happen to be true.

· FOUR ·
RELATIONSHIP TO THE ADVERSARIAL SYSTEM

You mentioned in your answer that we often describe trials—and I suppose you mean the whole of the adversarial system—as a search for truth and justice. I understand what you are saying about the representation of criminal defendants, but, that issue aside, isn't it true that lawyers are justified in what they do for their clients because they serve truth and justice by being a necessary part of the adversarial system? If so, don't we need to add something about that to our professional ideal?

The search for some combination of truth and justice is part of the function of the adversarial system. It is part of what that system is supposed to be about. I think, however, that we need to keep the functions of that system, and questions about its serving those functions, separate from our description of professionalism in the practice of law. Professionalism in the practice of law is about meaningful participation. That is a much broader concern than just being a part of the adversarial system. The adversarial system may make use of the participation we provide to try to produce its versions of truth and justice, and its other products, but that does not mean that the participation was about those products, or that it needs to be in order to be justified.

For example, each runner in a race is trying to win. The race itself is not about winning, however, but about entertainment. That does not change what the runner is about. The lead runner does not slow down to make the race more entertaining. In fact, if she does, if she confuses what the race is about with what she is about, she does damage to both. In sports, winning has its own value whether or not it serves well the value of entertainment.

Of course, the analogy is not complete, and I have done an injustice to all sports. Also, the analogy is a very unfortunate one for obvious reasons, but I think it makes the point. Participation is its own justification.

If you will permit me a lengthy aside, I said that the search for truth and justice is part of what the adversarial system is about. At the risk of sounding like an ideologue, much of the rest of what it is about is meaningful participation. It is not just a matter of coincidence that the adversarial system works best to produce truth and justice when there is meaningful participation by all parties and when the decision maker is keeping that participation meaningful by avoiding premature conclusions and by not prejudging the disputants. Providing meaningful participation is an important part of what the system is all about.

Even when the system is not working as it should to produce truth and justice, for example, when one attorney is not as capable of presenting the client's case as the opposing attorney, we seldom interfere with the participation the system affords to the disputants in the interests of pursuing truth and justice. Also, whether or not truth and justice is pursued through the adversarial system is left to the disputants, for the most part. The system has little interest in truth and justice when the disputants do not.

Part of the reason for the system's great deference to maximum participation by the disputants is that participation by them is essential to our perception of the fairness of the system, and our perception of its fairness is essential to its operation, both in the long run and in the short run. For example, it is essential to the operation of the system within our society that the disputants be reasonably willing to live with adverse judgments. Whether they are, or not, is dependent in part upon the perception of fairness which is, in turn, dependent in part upon the extent of their participation.[1]

I understand that your justification of professionalism does not depend on the truth and justice justification of the adversarial system. . . .

Or any other justification of it.

. . . Or any other, but surely the adversarial system limits the lawyer's professional obligations to his or her clients.

Yes, just like the runner, the lawyer has to play by the rules. The rules define permissible participation in the adversarial system just like criminal law defines permissible autonomy within a society. You have no professional obligation to do anything which violates those rules because society does not permit your client to participate in that way. You can describe that as a limit if you want to, but it seems to me to be no more than a reflection of the fact that the professional ideal is an ideal within a society as I said before.

So there is no obligation to the system other than to play by the rules? I have heard it said that lawyers are "officers of the court." Aren't there professional obligations that go along with that role?

First, as applied in case law, the expression usually means nothing more than that lawyers are subject to judicial regulation. Second, playing by the rules covers an awful lot of ground. Much of what people describe as our obligations as

---

1. *See* J. Thibault & L. Walker, *Procedural Justice, A Psychological Analysis* (1975).

officers of the court is no more than an obligation to play by the rules. Third, it seems to me, and I may be in the minority here, that all of the other obligations ascribed to the role of lawyers as officers of the court would be there even if we did not create that separate role for them. At one time or another, all of the following obligations have been attributed to our role as officers of the court: an obligation to represent indigent clients, an obligation to obey the law, and obligation to uphold the integrity and dignity of the legal system, an obligation to promote fair administration of justice, an obligation to be candid, an obligation to know the law, and an obligation to keep our clients informed.[2] I think all of those can come from a consistent application of our professional ideal of providing meaningful participation—most in obvious ways.

Even the Solicitor General's special obligations to the Supreme Court—he is spoken of as the Tenth Justice—are not obligations which are derived from the role of officer of that Court. They are derived from what his client, the "we" of "We, the people," want. The SG is asked to be non-political, to a certain extent, not because that is required by his office, but because it is required by his client. "Winning," in a political sense, is never an adequate description of what "we" want for there is much that we do not want our lawyer to do in order to win. For example, as I have said before about government lawyers, we do not want him to do anything inconsistent with our founding myth of the rule of law.

Fourth, most of the rules, customs, and so forth of the adversarial system are norms of cooperation and coordination that

---

2. This list is a modification of duties discussed in Martineau, "The Attorney as an Officer of The Court: Time to Take the Gown Off the Bar," 35 *S.C.L. Rev.* 541 (1984). The author makes the unfortunate mistake of saying that some of these obligations are unnecessary because they are found in the Code of Professional Responsibility. That is not an argument against the role of "officer" since some of the provisions of the Code are premised on that role. Nevertheless, the Article is instructive about the lack of need for the role.

make meaningful participation by the disputants within the system possible. They do not create much of a problem for our professional ideal.

I believe that *if* there are to be obligations to the adversarial system which impose institutional responsibilities upon lawyers *inconsistent* with our professional ideal, those obligations should be reduced to law through the normal processes.[3]

You are forewarned that this view is controversial. Most bar committees and commissions, both state and national, which have studied the subject of the professionalism of lawyers have recommended a reinvigoration of the role of officer of the court. I hope, and believe, that they are after the same things that I am. To me, however, the formation of a social role for lawyers which requires them to consider social interests other than those of our ideal of meaningful participation is an open invitation to confusion about the meaning of professionalism. The uniqueness of lawyers, that thing about them which makes it possible for them to serve the professional ideal, is that they are not officers of anything.

---

3. *See* Bell, "The Lawyer As Guardian," 11 *Soc. Resp.* 39 (Wash. & Lee 1985).

· FIVE ·
ETHICAL CODES AND PROFESSIONAL
ORGANIZATIONS

So you are still sticking with an obligation of service to one professional ideal?

Yes.

Isn't there an awful lot of growing tension in that professional ideal?

Yes, there is. In sticking with one professional ideal, I have moved much of the tension between the various other obligations that people ascribe to lawyers into the ideal of meaningful participation.

There is an inherent tension in the professionalism of lawyers. The concept calls for service to an ideal, but the ideal is a form of service to individuals. How can you serve the ideal and yet still serve the individual? It is as if the ideal keeps reflecting upon itself. In other words, the moral value we serve is personal autonomy, but service to personal autonomy conflicts with itself. You cannot provide personal autonomy by service to it as an ideal and yet, service to it as an ideal is a necessary condition for its existence in our society.

There is also a tension inherent in the concept of personal autonomy. I said before that one way of understanding how participation relates to personal autonomy is to understand personal autonomy as being the authoring of one's own life.

I also said that the moral value of personal autonomy was derived from the fact that there is a unique moral value in what it means to be you. There is a great tension between these two descriptions. You cannot be the author of your own meaning. You cannot give meaning to yourself. It is always a joint effort.

The expression "author one's own life" is a proud one, but you cannot live that way. Beyond the pride, there is a desperate loneliness in the circularity of the expression. There is much more to our concept of the individual than the one author.

All of this complexity about the individual, who is and isn't there, is unsettling for an ideal grounded in personal autonomy. Ironically, it is also the strength of the ideal. It shows, more clearly, the unique value of the meaning of each of us.

This is heady, and yet basic, stuff, but do you want to pursue it here? The real "tensions" as you describe them—those not created by misconceptions—will show up in any important dilemma you face as an attorney.

If the real tensions will show up anyhow, what is the point of your description of professionalism?

The point is that professionalism and good lawyering are one and the same and that good lawyering means, in part, being a good person. People who write about the practice of law often ask if it is possible to be a good lawyer and a good person. I want you to see that it is not only possible; it is difficult to avoid it. Of course, so far we have talked only about becoming good by doing good. There is much more to say about being a "good person" than that. Most people, however, are talking about "doing good" when they ask if a good lawyer can be a good person.

Another point is that our profession is a service to private ends. I want you to see that our professionalism makes that a public calling.

I am worried about those dilemmas you mentioned. How will I go about resolving the ethical dilemmas I will face as an attorney?

I hope that thinking carefully about professionalism will help. Aside from that, there is an abundance of guidance available to you—some of it very good and some of it not—from our professional organizations.

Do you mean our ethical codes?

Yes, in part. Unfortunately, through what may be an unavoidable evolutionary process, our codes have become more concerned with the profession and less concerned with professionalism.

What do you mean? What evolutionary process?

An evolution from morals to ethics to ethical regulation to rules of law. It is an evolution moving constantly in the direction of increasing coerciveness and, as it does, necessarily reducing the profession's guidance from aspiration to minimally acceptable conduct. We went very quickly from what not to be to what not to do.[1]

The latest steps in this evolution, as you know or will soon find out, are the elimination of the "Ethical Considerations" of the American Bar Association Code of Professional Conduct, which were supposed to be "aspirational in character and represent[ing] the objectives towards which every member of the profession should strive"[2] in the adoption by the Amer-

---

1. The expression is from Hitchler, "The Physical Elements of Crime," 39 *Dick. L. Rev.* 95 (1935) (citing L. Stephen, *The Science Of Ethics* 148 (2d ed. [1907]).

2. "Preliminary Statement," *Model Code of Professional Responsibility* (1981).

ican Bar Association of the Model Rules of Professional Conduct and the structuring of the Model Rules as rules of law.

What is wrong with rules which articulate clearly the standards of minimally acceptable conduct?

Nothing. In fact, there is something very good about the clear articulation of rules which are the bases for imposing sanctions, and there is something very right about attorneys considering their conduct in light of the shared norms of the profession even if the norms are minimum standards of conduct. The problem is that it is very difficult for attorneys to stay clear about the role of the rules, and about what attorneys are, and are not, doing when they conform their conduct to the rules. It is easy, in other words, to confuse compliance with the rules with being moral and it is easy to confuse minimally acceptable conduct with acting as a professional.

What do you mean? Why is it so difficult for lawyers?

We get used to thinking about rules in a particular way. Part of what you learned, or are learning, in the first year of law school is to argue not from your own values, but from the values of the law. Part of the trauma of the first year experience is this required shift from the judge inside to the judge outside as the source of decisions. It is a shift from you to a legal community in order to be able to argue within that community from shared meanings.

Some students never learn that lesson, and, what is worse, some students never forget it.

The judge outside is a hypothetical, authoritative, decision maker whom, we assume, thinks about disputes in a particular way. The shift in our perspective to that of this judge outside shapes the way we think about rules and the way we talk to each other about them.[3] It is one way of thinking about the

---

3. *See* the Appendix, part 2, for a further discussion of ways to think about the law.

law, but it won't do as a way of thinking about professionalism. If I approach the rules of the profession as rules of law, their meaning for me becomes a prediction as to how the judge outside would apply them. That meaning is a meaning created within the framework of a particular historical context and within a particular legal community. The problem is that professionalism requires that we move the judge back inside, and, when we do, the entire process collapses back on itself. Thinking about the rules of the profession as rules of law is good for determining when and how society will intervene in my actions, but it is not good for determining how I should judge them.

Let me give you an example at my own expense. Look again at my "resolution" of the Second Guarantee Clause hypothetical. I asked: Does this fall under the category of "dishonesty" which denies meaningful participation to the other party? The problem with that formulation of the question is that, if I take it too far, it is nonsense. I, alone, will decide what the word "dishonesty" means simultaneous with my determination of what facts are sufficient to constitute "dishonesty."

If the word "dishonesty" was taken from an ethical code, such as in Directory Rule 1-102(A)(4) of the Code of Professional Responsibility ("A lawyer shall not . . . engage in conduct involving dishonesty. . . . "), and I wanted to know what it meant, I could—admittedly with great difficulty in this example—argue with others about that from an evolving shared meaning for the word because the hypothetical, authoritative, decision maker provides the historical and community contexts within which that shared meaning can evolve. But when the argument is not with another, but with myself—the conversation of the "two-in-one" in Hannah Arendt's phrase[4]—I cannot argue from meaning because I, alone, will determine meaning. I must think about the problem anew from the continuities of who I am, my morality, my thought processes, etc.

---

4. H. Arendt, *The Life Of The Mind* 171-93 (1971).

The word "dishonesty" can help focus my attention on what is important in the problem, but it cannot serve as a substitute for my thinking. I have to stay alive in the dilemma.

That's difficult to do, isn't it? Don't you keep bumping into great uncertainty?

Yes, and yes. What did you expect? Of course, it is difficult, but then so are most virtues. And, after all, is this so different than asking the Statute of Frauds client to consider something other than the legality of his proposed conduct? To approach professionalism as if it was something outside of you, as the law is something outside of you, is to leave the morality of professionalism behind.

But if what you are describing is too difficult, people won't do it.

You may be right. There are a lot of things I could say to reassure you that it is not as difficult as it may seem, but I do not want to, yet. We are back at the question of whether or not our professional ideal is realistic enough to serve as an ideal. We are still talking about an ideal.

If it is difficult, why can't I get more help with it from the rules of the profession. why have they evolved to minimum standards of conduct?

As I said before, we have moved constantly in the direction of increasing coercion and, when we do that, we have to reduce our standards to what can be accomplished through coercion. One of the primary values of our rules is that they can reduce the problem of competitive disadvantage.[5] For

---

5. Luban, "Calming the Hearse Horse: A Philosophical Research Program for Legal Ethics," 40 *Md. L. Rev.* 451, 461 (1981). *See also* Davis, "The Moral Authority of The Professional Code," in J. Rennock and J. Chapman, eds., *Authority Revisited: NOMOS XXI* 97.

example, lying in negotiation provides such an advantage that the possibility of one side lying creates a strong incentive for the other side to lie as well. If you reduce the possibility, you reduce the incentive. One way of reducing the possibility is through the threat of coercively enforced rules. For the rules to have that effect, however, they must be perceived as a realistic threat. That need moves the rules towards minimum standards of conduct. The rules can't be too general or too aspirational.

It all sounds rather nasty.

It is.

Why don't we rely on other methods of reducing the possibility?

We seem to be losing our belief in the efficacy of the other ways. We do not trust each other, in other words. I suppose the reason for that has something to do with loss of community, changing demographics, etc. At least, those are the usual explanations. The question is too big for me.

I think much of the recent attention on professionalism can be seen as one effort to reform our legal community and I think we can judge the work of the ABA and state bar associations in that regard by whether or not they move us in the direction of community.

Organizations like the ABA and state bar associations are important to professionalism, but they are also a threat to it.

I understand how they are important. How are they a threat?

It is difficult for an organization to maintain the self-reflection needed for professionalism. It is difficult for it to maintain a "vantage point for its critique."[6] The organization is depen-

---

6. The phrase is from Fish, "Anti-Professionalism," 7 *Cardozo L. Rev.* 645, 677 (1986).

dent on us, as individuals, to maintain a distance from the profession if the profession is to act in the spirit of professionalism. In essence, our professional ideal is a uniquely individual one; not an institutional one.

I know that must sound terribly abstract and I know that you realize that it can be read on many different levels. Remember when I said that you had to make moral judgments about serving our professional ideal in particular situations if the ideal is to remain a moral one? In other words, you had to transcend the ideal to be true to it. It may help to think that way about our organizations.

Can you give an example?

The Code of Professional Responsibility was drafted in the late '60s by well-meaning professionals. In 1977, Professor Tom Morgan, then at the University of Illinois, wrote an article entitled "The Evolving Concept of Professional Responsibility"[7] in which he analyzed the Code from the perspective of the interests it served. It was Professor Morgan's conclusion that the Code inverted "the proper ranking" of the interests we should serve as a profession. In essence, he said that the Code placed the interests of lawyers first.

Whether Professor Morgan was correct in his analysis, and whether the interests he identified are the interests we should serve, and whether *his* "proper ranking" is *the* proper ranking are all questions which are beside the point of his article as an example. What Professor Morgan did in the article is offer a "vantage point for critique" outside of the profession.[8] It is a vantage point based on the quality of our relationship as a profession to those we serve. It is a vantage point based on an ideal disciplined by reason, in my opinion, and I believe it came from within Professor Morgan. Basically, his article is a

---

7. Morgan, "The Evolving Concept of Professional Responsibility," 90 *Harv. L. Rev.* 702 (1977).

8. *See* the Appendix, part 3, for more discussion.

call to the profession to be truly professional, as we have defined it, and the profession continues to respond to that call.

The example is a simplistic one, but I think it may make the point.

Are you saying that we need to watch out for our professional organizations?

No, I am saying that we have to maintain a personal distance from our profession—a distance which permits moral judgment.

This is pure opinion—and I want you to form your own on the subject—but I believe our organizations feel the call of professionalism very strongly and that they have been responsive to it.

Despite your good opinion of them, I think you are saying that it is difficult for our organizations to maintain a professional distance from the profession.

Yes, I am.

If that is true, then why are we permitted to govern ourselves? Isn't that asking for trouble?

Yes, it is. Part of the answer is that we are governed by the judiciary to a large extent. The rest of the answer is that, to the extent that we do govern ourselves, the trouble we ask for if others govern us is greater.

Why? What do you mean?

As I have said before, our uniqueness, that thing about us which makes it possible for us to serve a professional ideal based on individual autonomy, is that we are not officers of anything. We serve private ends and, as I have tried to show, that is a public service. But we cannot serve the public directly, as I believe we would be called upon to do if we were not self-governing, and still serve private ends. I think you have seen in our discussion how easy it is for our professional obligation of service to individuals to be usurped into service to something else.

Please do not think that I am saying that we see the needs of society more clearly than others or that we have some kind of monopoly on understanding the value of our professional ideal or its meaning. What I am trying to say is that the discussion of who is to govern is a discussion which is not about lawyers doing a better job, but whether or not we will have lawyers at all.

As you can see, I believe that some degree of professional autonomy is necessary for professionalism—at least for our professionalism. That autonomy imposes upon our profession a difficult responsibility. Our freedom to choose is an enormous limitation on us.

· SIX ·

THE IMAGE OF OUR PROFESSION

You said that we have no monopoly on understanding the value of our professional ideal. If that is true, and if others can understand it, why don't they rally behind us? Why are we so disliked as a profession?

There have been a lot of answers given to that question. One of the most frequent answers is that we are condemned by association.

What do you mean?

The public associates us with our client—particularly our unpopular ones. They do that to such an extent that one study has determined that our association with criminal defendants is the primary cause of our lack of popularity.

We are associated with the law and with its coerciveness. In our society, "I am going to call my lawyer" means that "I am going to call upon the law to make you do what I want you to do." We are associated with the slipperiness of rules of law. To the public, the law makes a black art out of common sense notions of wrong and right.[1] We are also associated with the law's natural conservativeness, and its tendency to side with the "haves" in battles with the "have-nots."

---

1. K. Llewellyn, *The Bramble Bush* 145 (1960).

We are associated with institutions which have fallen on hard times. We are associated with the adversarial system and with its abuses. We are associated with a form of procedural justice that is heavy on procedure and light on justice. We are also associated with complexity, the complexity of our society which is reflected directly in our laws and in our legal systems.

Some have said that we are not to be blamed for these causes of our lack of popularity because it is condemnation by association, and some have said that we are not to be blamed because:

> Apart from procedure, and touching the charges which remain: as to the twisting of rules to win; as to there being no gain at law except at the flat expense of trampling, of putting the boot to a loser; as to the longer purse holding unfair advantage; as to the closed ranks of the law in favor of what is—surely three-fourths of the sting of the charges is drawn, and mud clapped on the wound, when one looks to the obvious truth: that in these matters law and lawyers do not show themselves, distinctly, . . . at all. In these matters the lawyer's mirror undistorted the very society that makes the charge.[2]

The author of that passage, Karl Llewellyn, blames us only for the "mangled mass of most procedure"[3] and for a system of dispute resolution which "tends to make lawyers forget their client's interest in their own and to forget in both the interest—if such there be—of justice."[4]

Those who speak that way raise my suspicions. That answer to your question leads nowhere. It says that this is just the way things are and that we suffer from it because people do not understand the good we do. Llewellyn's defense of the profession is a self-proclaimed martyrdom. I do not know of

---

2. *Id.*
3. *Id.*
4. *Id.*

any successful self-proclaimed martyrs, and I don't believe anyone will be proclaimed a martyr by others when his message is: "I know what is best for you." Llewellyn's message to me is that we are, in fact, practitioners of a black art that only we can fully appreciate. He says that: "Singers of songs and dreamers of plays—even though they be lawyers—build a house no wind blows over."[5] But when he is called upon to describe our "house," it is the law, the adversarial system, and procedural justice he describes—all of those associates whose guilt we share in the public eye. I think the public could respond that our song is off-key and our play is closing off-Broadway. In other words, "What you say is best for us, isn't." I believe that the "gentle cynicism"[6] of the people will not permit lawyer-heroes of the sort Llewellyn describes.

Nevertheless, I am sure that there is truth in what he says. I am also sure that it is a truth that does not do us much good. I want to answer your question with other causes for our poor image.

Now that you have told me what the answer isn't, what is it?

I think that our poor image is caused, in part—the part important for us as individuals—by our lack of professionalism, and I do not blame that lack, as Llewellyn does, on our "trial by combat" system of justice.[7]

It is far too easy and too attractive to look back on the long history of antagonism towards lawyers and to see that antagonism as inevitable. But that story about our profession is just an excuse. As individuals, I think that it is better to confront the ways in which we may contribute to our poor image.

---

5. *Id.*

6. Shaffer, "The Ethics of Dissent and Friendship in the American Professions," 88 *W. Va. L. Rev.* 623, 648 (1986).

7. K. Llewellyn, *supra* note 1, at 145.

How do we contribute to our poor image?

Part of our contribution is that we do not do what Llewellyn says we do. We do not mirror society because we do not mirror who our clients are in their disputes. Too often, the participation we provide does not "reflect and reflect upon" the person of the client. Too often, the image of the client presented by the lawyer to society and the image of society presented by the lawyer to the client is badly distorted by the lawyer. We tend to remake both our clients and our society in our own worst images of them.

What is our own worst image of them?

We present an image of clients to society as people who seek only to maximize their selfish interests with any available means, and we go back to our clients with an image of a society which requires that.

Why do we do that?

Well, one reason is that it makes our lives so much easier. Those images are licenses to act without consideration of the complexities of our professional obligations. Those images also allow us to maintain a belief in our own superiority—something we sometimes think is required to be comfortable with thinking of ourselves as professionals. There is something else to it as well. There is something in the nature of formal roles of service to others that makes the server want to demean those who are served. Why that is is a question for others. There is no doubt, however, that the professionalism I am trying to describe requires the lawyer to give up the security of formal roles, and to escape that institutional trap. That is part of what I meant when I said, back in the beginning, that the lawyer and the client must constantly redefine what it means to be a lawyer for this client in this dispute.

What can I do about that?

For one, you can learn to recognize the problem and its many symptoms. That alone is an enormous task. Cynicism about people and about society is deeply ingrained in many of the images we have of ourselves. As you read about your profession, look for implicit cynical images of people and of society. What is implied, for example, when we equate "high quality" or "good" lawyering with proficiency in maximizing selfish interests through any available means? Look out for implicit images of our clients as children who never learned that they cannot have everything their own way. Look out for those who think that clients cannot accept the fact that they may be wrong on the merits and who try to preserve for the client a self-image of one who is always right by blaming events on various scapegoats such as the legal system, the judge, or— most favored of all—the lawyer on the other side. That need to explain away events rather than acknowledging responsibility for them is a telling symptom of a lack of client participation in the dispute. Watch out for it. Clients cannot act autonomously, they cannot become who they are, if we separate them from the consequences of their thoughts and their acts. The lawyer who thinks that he is helping a client by hiding him from who he is, is wrong. Watch out for those who describe our society and our legal system for their clients and who do not realize that the client can choose for himself what the "rules of the game" will be for him. In other words, watch out for those who do not realize that describing society, and our legal system, is a moral act in which the client is entitled to participate.

How will all that help our image?

I believe that the only way that we can get people to appreciate what we do is to do it. All of the problems that I am asking you to recognize are examples of lawyers who are not practicing law as professionals, as we have defined that term.

· SEVEN ·
BEING A PROFESSIONAL

It looks to me that the professional ideal you have described is far too demanding. You have made professionalism too inaccessible, haven't you?

That is the question of whether the ideal is realistic enough to serve as an ideal seen from the perspective of an individual. No one wants to be set up for failure, and I understand your concern.

In my answer to your first question about the meaning of professionalism, I said that professionalism was serving others in a manner which approaches a professional ideal. "Manner" is an important part of that definition. You cannot find a successful "manner" of service to others by deriving rules of conduct from our professional ideal because our ideal, as I have said before, is full of tensions. The ideal cannot resolve those tensions for you. You cannot resolve all of the dilemmas you will face as a lawyer by asking what an abstract "ideal lawyer" would do, and, in that sense, you cannot be successful in becoming a good lawyer by trying to model your conduct after the ideal. Our ideal is, as you have said, inaccessible.

But professionalism is not inaccessible. When I spoke of a "manner" of serving others, I was speaking not of an ethic of principle—which is what we have been discussing—but of an ethic of character. Because of the tensions within our ideal, professionalism as an ethic of principle ultimately collapses into an ethic of character. Doing something in a certain manner is doing it with a certain character. It is a "way of being in all circumstances."[1] You cannot resolve the tensions in our professional ideal by seeking the ideal, but only by seeking what is right. Your seeking what is right is informed by principle, but it is achieved by character. In one sense, all that I am saying is that you are ultimately responsible for being a professional and determining what that means. You cannot cast that responsibility off to a professional ideal. It is yours, and it is yours right now.

Unlike an ethic of principle, an ethic of character is not an ethic of success or failure in living up to an ideal of conduct.[2] Conversations about character are conversations about real people, not abstract ideals, and those conversations accept failure as they do success in an "unfailing respect for the humanity of . . . all men."[3] The tensions in our professional ideal are not invitations for failure, when viewed from this perspective, but opportunities for character. Those opportunities leave room for you as you leave room for your clients by providing opportunities for character in their disputes. (You will discover, I believe, that when you achieve character in your decisions, your clients will have achieved it with you, quite suddenly.)

There is room for you in our profession. There is no role waiting for you to fill it—no ethical model into whose contours you must squeeze. There is only what you will create. Accepting the responsibility of that is professionalism.[4]

---

1. S. R. Letwin, *The Gentlemen in Trollope* 268 (1982) (cited in T. Shaffer, *American Legal Ethics: Text, Reading, and Discussion Topics* 57 (1985) [hereinafter *Gentlemen*].

2. *See* T. Shaffer, *American Legal Ethics: Text, Readings, and Discussion Topics* 70-74 (1985). *See also* Elkins, "Ethics: Professionalism, Craft, and Failure," 73 *Kent. L. Rev.* 945 (1985) for the role of failure in an ethic of craft applied to professionalism.

3. *Gentlemen, supra*, note 1 at 268.

4. For a look at what the A.B.A. Commission on Professionalism had to say to law schools about their role in this process, see the Appendix, part 4.

Do you get the last word?

No. Go ahead.

I think that there are other professional ideals and that there are other values which conflict with the ones asserted by your professional ideal.

You may be right. Tell me about it.

APPENDIX

PART 1

In the text, I have said that the moral value of autonomy is derived from a moral assertion about the individual—for each person we can say that there is a unique morality in what it means to be "you." In the footnote, I have said that there are many ways of understanding that assertion. One way of doing so is as Alasdair MacIntyre does, as the "unity of a narrative embodied in a single life" which provides the context for meaning. A. MacIntyre, *After Virtue*, 2nd ed., 218 (1984).

We can also understand this moral assertion as a good for each individual which allows us to understand why a moral life is a good one, not only for the individual, but also for man. Here is one description of the good of one's identity:

> "There is this good that consists not merely in my being a human being of a certain sort but in my being and continuing to be who I am. The goods that are (so far as possible) thrown away in suicide include that good. It is closely related to, but analytically distinguishable from, the good which Nozick rightly points out is thrown away by plugging in to the experience machine [a machine which feeds pleasure experiences, chosen by you, to your brain] viz. the good of being a person of a certain sort, that good which Nozick has in mind when he asks 'Why should we be concerned only with how our time is filled, but not with what we are?' I think

Aristotle's principle [that no one chooses to possess the whole world if he has first to become someone else] is concerned not only with the good of being 'what we are' (i.e., of being what we, as beings with a certain nature, can be), but also with the good, for each one of us, of being who one is.

In reflecting on this principle, we are near bedrock. But at least two lines of thought seem to contribute to it. One is an understanding of the givenness of one's place in the cosmos, and indeed of one's self; to lose one's identity would thus be, in a sense, to lose (willingly or unwillingly) the priceless gift with which one began and which all other attainments can only supplement. The other is . . . : all one's free choices go to constitute oneself, so that one's own character or identity is the most fundamental of one's accomplishments'; the accomplishment most unequivocally one's own; and if one's character is bad there still remains the possibility of a repentance and reformation which will be as much one's own accomplishment as one's former, regrettable, accomplishments . . . ." J. Finnis, *Fundamentals of Ethics* 40 (1983).

By making a moral assertion about the individual as the premise of professionalism, I am really saying very little. There should be little baggage attached to that assertion. I certainly am not saying that the individual is prior, in any sense, to society. In fact, as should be clear in the later chapters of the text, I believe that it is thinking *that* way about the individual, and about society, that gets us into trouble in the first place in our understanding of the practice of law.

PART 2

Thinking of the law as an object outside of us is a view of convenience here. Do not let me restrict you. Thinking of the law that way narrowly defines law and law-making activities. If you broaden the definitions, the distinction I am making here becomes much less clear.

It is possible to see the law as a much more participatory process. In very real and practical ways, we create law in our conversations about disputes. Adjudication of legal disputes can be viewed as acts of interpretation and not of coercion. Thinking of adjudication that way is helpful to me in understanding how a person is reflected in the resolution of a legal dispute. Nevertheless, I believe that there is an imperative core of adjudication and that we can place law outside of us to criticize it from a variety of moral and ethical perspectives. Here is one explication of that position which may whet your appetite for more of this debate:

> "By focusing on the distinctively imperative core of adjudication, instead of its interpretive gloss, we free up meaningful criticism of law. Adjudication, like all of law, is imperative—it is a part of politics. Politics, like all of history, is contingent—it is part of that which is—and interpretation of law is and should be grounded in this historical, contingent, and positive text. The criticism of law, by contrast, must be grounded in a different text. It cannot be grounded in yet another interpretation of that which is. It must rest on a claim regarding that which ought to be, not a claim regarding that which is, or how power has been used to date. It must be grounded in the text we didn't write—the text of our natural needs, our true potential, our utopian ideals. Criticism of law must be grounded in the natural and ideal text, not the contingent text, if it is to be truly critical.
>
> How do we, or should we, criticize an act of power? In public life, no less than in private life, I believe we should criticize acts of power not by reference to their rationality, or their coherency, or their 'integrity,' but by reference to their motivation and their effects. An act of power in public life as well as in private life that is pra-

iseworthy is an act of power which, in short, is loving: it is the act that originates in the heart and is prompted by our sympathy for the needs of others, and empathy for their situation. I see no reason not to hold adjudicatory acts of power to this standard. *Brown v. Board of Education*, for example, is a good opinion, because it is a sympathetic rather than cynical response to a cry of pain, not because it renders 'consistent' conflicting strands of constitutional jurisprudence. Indeed, the strength of the opinion lies more in its willingness to ignore the community's texts rather than its willingness to read them: the opinion speaks to our real need for fraternity rather than our expressed xenophobia; and it taps our real potential for an enlarged community and an enlarged conception of self rather than our expressed fear of differences. The test of the morality of power in public life as in private life may be neither compliance with community mores, as objectivists insist, nor political success, as subjectivists claim, but love. Imperativism, distinctively, frees the critic for this possibility." West, "Adjudication Is Not Interpretation: Some Reservations About The Law-As-Literature Movement," 54 *Tenn. L. Rev.* 230, 278 (1981). (Footnote omitted.)

The distinction of the judge inside from the judge outside also breaks down somewhat in Kantian ethics on the "inside" part of the distinction. Kant believed that the inside judge— the voice of conscience—must be presumed to be the voice of another. The voice of conscience speaks of moral law derived from reason but, if the voice is not the voice of another, that moral law can be rationalized away. Kant's hypothetical inside judge is very similar to the hypothetical outside judge, and a distinction in those thinking processes is difficult to maintain. The authority of the inside judge and the application of what he says are difficult subjects in Kant far beyond our purposes here. I do want you to realize, however, that the inside judge and outside judge distinction I make in the text is not an obvious one at all.

PART 3

There are those who say that we are not capable of finding true "vantage points of critique" from which we can criticize our profession. *See*, Fish, "Anti-Professionalism," 7 *Cardozo L. Rev.* 645 (1986). And there are many other ways of describing the role of critic than the way I have chosen here. We have stumbled here into a currently raging debate between liberals (in the philosophical, and not the political sense) and communitarians (in the same sense). There is much to be learned from this debate. *See, e.g.*, "The Many Faces of Jurisprudence: A Symposium," 54 *Tenn. L. Rev.* 161 (1987). And our discussion of professionalism can offer you a way of approaching that debate as something other than an intellectual exercise.

The questions asked in that debate are questions about some of the assumptions I have used in describing professionalism, particularly assumptions about the person of the client and about the nature of morality. You can approach this debate instrumentally, if you want to, to see how each side can help you formulate your own conception of the meaning of the profession. Of course, this debate cannot tell you which side is right, if either side is, and you should not expect that. At its heart, the debate is a reflection on the nature of man and our reflections on ourselves will always be as suspect as any self-reflecting statements are. But this debate is far from an exercise in futility. This debate can be very relevant to your personal judgments of what is right.

For my purposes, the liberal view of man necessarily misdescribes the interconnectivity of the individual and society, and the communitarian view does the same. The radical "I" is a "we," and the radical "we" is an "I." Even in the simple example I make of Professor Morgan's article I would argue that his criticism of the profession is not just one of logical inconsistency or just a view from a different social perspective, but is based on a nature which individuals can use as "a moral text for criticism of social life." West, "Adjudication Is Not

Interpretation: Some Reservations About The Law-As-Litera-ture Movement," 54 *Tenn L. Rev.* 203, 207 (1987). But the "individual" I have in mind is not the lonely, ahistorical, and circular entity of so much of liberal thought. It is an individual defined, in part, by a community and a history. In other words, I think that we can have it both ways.

I have offered bare bone assertions here to provoke you to further inquiry, and to ask you to see that jurisprudential questions like these can be immediately relevant to you as a law student or as a lawyer.

Without the puzzle of the meaning of our profession I am afraid that I would have had a harder time understanding the practical relevance of this debate. I hope the puzzles in this book can offer you a way into this debate as well and into other jurisprudential debates. I believe that one of the most theoretical courses you can take in law school will be a good clinic, and one of the most practical will be a good course in jurisprudence. I encourage you to do both, if you have not already done so, and to continue exploring our profession from those complementary perspectives.

PART 4

If you are a law student, one part of your responsibility is to think critically about the models of lawyering offered to you in law school. Here is what the A.B.A. Commission on Professionalism had to say on that subject:

"Law professors, along with practicing lawyers, serve as important, early examples for law students of what constitutes proper professional behavior. Law professors can transmit the wrong message through their manner and conduct both inside and outside the classroom. The first image that law students may receive is that the most successful lawyers are those who provide fast repartee and use the Socratic method with facility. As Dean Norman Redlich of New York University Law School told members of the Commission, 'As a client, I would want an attorney who was deliberative and did not immediately respond with the first idea that came to mind and who did not attempt through the course of the conference to prove his or her brilliance.'

Other, more troubling, signals can be sent to students. These include a lack of respect for the views of others and a lack of commitment to providing *pro bono* services. As former Dean Erwin Griswold of Harvard observed, law students frequently come to law school with broader ideals than they take out. And, he emphasized, this is not due to a loss of innocence or naivete by the students so much as to a diminution of their desire, as seen by example, to serve society.

Unquestionably, an important mission of law schools must be the teaching of professionalism and the setting of proper role models for law students. If there is a lack of adequate role models in law schools, lawyers may begin practice with little sense of the responsibilities to a client and to society inherent in a professional relationship.

Of course, the sensitizing of law students about ethical issues is not only the responsibility of law schools. Often, law students' first exposure to the world of practicing lawyers comes when they clerk for law firms at the end of their first year in law school and thereafter. If what they see in these firms is inconsistent with the ideals taught in law school, the best academic effort may be for naught. The education process is an 'ongoing' one for which all segments of the profession, not just the law schools, must take responsibility." " ... In The Spirit of Public Service: 'A Blueprint For The Rekindling of Lawyer Professionalism," *American Bar Association Commission On Professionalism* 19 (1986).